HOW

TO   REMEMBER

ANYTHING

Other DEAN VAUGHN Memory Products

The Vaughn Cube for Music Theory

The Vaughn Cube for World Geography

How to Master the Art of Public Speaking and Speech Communication

The Vaughn Cube for Addition / Subtraction

The Vaughn Cube for Multiplication / Division

The Vaughn Cube for Plane and Solid Geometry Formulas

How to Learn and Remember the Periodic Table

Instant Spanish—Conversational Spanish Course (CD-ROM)

How to Learn and Remember 1000 Spanish Vocabulary Words

How to Tell Time

U.S. Memory Map Puzzle

How to Learn and Remember the Books of the Bible

Latin and Greek for English Vocabulary and SAT Verbal Mastery

Academic and business site licenses for the following
Dean Vaughn Total Retention Courses are available
exclusively through DCM Instructional Systems,
a division of DCM Systems, Incorporated:

Medical Terminology 350

Basic Human Anatomy

Dental Terminology, Anatomy, and Physiology

For more information or a free video demo, please visit
www.deanvaughn.com.

HOW
TO REMEMBER
ANYTHING

The
Proven Total
Memory Retention
System

DEAN VAUGHN

 St. Martin's Griffin New York

www.stmartins.com

Design by Susan Walsh

Illustrations courtesy of Dean Vaughn Learning Systems, Inc.

Library of Congress Cataloging-in-Publication Data

Vaughn, Dean E.
    How to remember anything : the proven total memory retention system / Dean Vaughn.—
1st ed.
        p. cm.
    ISBN-13: 978-0-312-36734-3
    ISBN-10: 0-312-36734-1
    1. Mnemonics.   2. Memory.   I. Title.

BF385.V38 2007
153.1'4—dc22

2007005728

10   9   8   7   6   5

I dedicate this book to the millions of individuals throughout the world who have completed my applied memory courses. Because of their unprecedented successes, surely organized memory techniques will soon become as much a part of formal education as reading, writing, and arithmetic. They have added the "fourth R"—remembering!

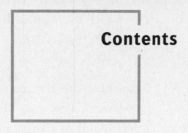

Contents

PART II: MORE PRACTICAL APPLICATIONS

YOU CAN REMEMBER ANYTHING!

*Memory is power! Without memory, no knowledge can exist. You can rap-*idly develop your memory to a phenomenal degree if you have a sincere desire to do so. No learned skill can be so easily or dramatically developed as the memory. You are about to discover that you can increase your memory power to a phenomenal degree in just ten easy steps. Various combinations of these ten steps will make it possible for you to rapidly learn and remember virtually anything, no matter how complex the information may be! This book includes the basic methods of my learning system, enabling you to apply it to your own specific needs. If you spend an average of only ten to fifteen minutes per day for just several weeks learning these ten simple steps, you will be amazed and excited about your new-found memory power!

In just minutes from now, when you learn the numbered room system, you will see how this organized memory system can work for you. Although the numbered room system is just the first step, it has many applications. You will start slowly, then expand to more complex applications. However, all of the memory techniques will be just as easy as learning the numbered room system.

With more than two and a half million individuals having completed my courses with an average of more than 95 percent retention, I can confidently assure you that you will remember incredibly more of what you need to remember because you will be seeing rather than reading or hearing. My learning system is based on your natural ability to remember exceptionally well the things that you see—even if what you see is only in your mind's eye—and I'll show you how to change anything you want to remember into something you can see. Then I'll show you how to connect what you see with something you already know. That's it! It's never any more difficult than that! Even if the information is complex, you will always use only two objects at a time. One object or familiar physical location will represent what you already know and the other will represent what you want to remember.

The memory skills taught in this book will help you achieve more in less time than you have ever dreamed possible. They will arm you with a competitive edge that others do not have (unless they have also discovered the secrets revealed in this book). You will be able to put these skills into practical use immediately. They will help you stay mentally alert for a lifetime.

The purpose of this book is to teach you how to remember anything—quickly, easily, and accurately. I will guide you step-by-step to phenomenal memory power! Rather than boring you with the history of memory techniques, how the brain works, why we forget, or philosophical reasons as to why you should develop your memory skills, I will teach you how to remember. After all, that must surely be the reason you are reading this book.

Achieving results with the well-organized, dramatically effective learning systems you will discover in this book will be one of the most rewarding experiences of your life. It will also be one of the most exciting and enjoyable. Additionally, you can use the techniques for the rest of your life. Use your natural memory and common sense in every memory application. Your natural memory, working in harmony with common sense and effective memory techniques, will enable you to achieve phenomenal results. Trust the system. I promise that you will be surprised and very pleased with your results.

Part I

THE TEN STEPS TO HOW TO REMEMBER ANYTHING

Step 1

A NUMBERED ROOM SYSTEM

As you read this chapter, place yourself in a square or rectangular room. If you are not, just visualize a very familiar room that is square or rectangular. Any room with four walls, four corners, a floor, and a ceiling will work. That's ten locations.

There are only ten single-digit numbers—zero through nine. I am going to permanently assign the ten single-digit numbers to the ten basic locations of any square or rectangular room.

Visualize yourself at the center of the room, and turn so that you are facing the front wall of the room. Any wall can be chosen to represent the front wall of the room.

As you look at the following illustration of the numbered room locations, look, also, at the corresponding room locations in the room in which you are now located or the room that you are visualizing.

As you look at the illustration, note that the four corners are odd numbers: 1, 3, 5, and 7. They start in the back left corner, and move clockwise to the corners around the room:

Back left corner is location 1
Front left corner is location 3

Front right corner is location 5
Back right corner is location 7

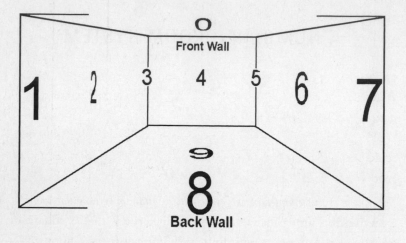

The four walls of the room are the even numbers: 2, 4, 6, and 8. They start at the left wall, and move clockwise to the walls around the room:

Left wall is location 2
Front wall is location 4
Right wall is location 6
Back wall is location 8

The ceiling of the room is location 0 and the floor is location 9.

I suggest that you put this book down and look around the room. Look at all the locations, starting with 0 at the ceiling, then 1, 2, 3, and so on. Then look at them in reverse order. Last, look at each location randomly and think of the number assigned to it.

You now have a memory bank for the numbers 0 through 9.

Before continuing, please be certain you know the ten numbered room locations. For example, when you think of number 7, you should immediately think of the back right corner of the room. If you think of number 2, you should immediately think of the left wall.

You should be able to close your eyes and see each of the ten locations forward, backward, or randomly. You should also be able to think of any number between 0 and 9 and quickly see its room location in your mind.

I call this numbered room system a Cube, even though you will seldom be in a room that is actually a cube. This numbered Cube methodology has been used in thousands of academic and corporate applications with unprecedented success.

Let's suggest that you want to learn and remember information in which a numbered sequence is important. For example, let's use the first nine presidents of the United States. The information you want to remember could be any numbered sequence. Please follow the steps very carefully, even if you are not interested in the content. The content is not what is important. What's important is to know how the system works so you can use it in almost limitless practical applications.

I mentioned earlier that all of my memory techniques include only two objects at a time. One object represents what you already know and the other represents what you want to remember. Both must be objects or locations you can see. In this case, you already know the nine numbered locations in the Cube. We will not use the 0 location (ceiling) for this exercise. You can actually see or visualize each of the nine locations, so these are your knowns or what you already know.

What you want to remember is the name of the president for each of the nine numbered locations. That means the name of each president must be converted to something you can see. To do this,

I'll change the name of each president to a soundalike picture, as follows:

President	Sounds Like or Suggests
Washington	washing machine
Adams	(newspaper) ad
Jefferson	chef (the object is based on sound, not on spelling)
Madison	medicine
Monroe	money
Adams	(newspaper) ad
Jackson	(automobile) jack
Van Buren	van
Harrison	hair

Be certain that you know the soundalike picture for each of the presidents before continuing.

The next step is to associate each soundalike picture with its numbered Cube location. This will automatically give you the numerical sequence of each president.

Look at location 1 (the back left corner). As you look at location 1, see a gigantic washing machine filling the entire corner! Imagine that the washing machine is running, the lid is open, and water and wet clothing is pouring out all over you!

Later, when you think of number 1—the first president—think of location 1, the back left corner. See the *washing machine* and remember Washington.

Look at location 2 (the left wall). As you look at the left wall, see a gigantic ad—a newspaper ad! Later, when you think of number 2, think of location 2—the left wall. See the *ad* and remember Adams, the second president.

Look at location 3 (the front left corner). See a chef standing in the corner! The chef reaches from the floor to the ceiling! If you were ever to see this in real life, how could you ever forget it? Later, when you think of number 3, think of location 3—the front left corner. See the *chef* and remember Jefferson.

Look at location 4—the front wall. As you look at the front wall, see medicine pouring out of it! It is liquid medicine and it is really messy. Imagine the medicine pouring out of the front wall all over you! Later, when you think of number 4, think of location 4—the front wall. See the *medicine* and remember Madison.

Next, look at location 5 (the front right corner). See money bursting out of the front right corner of the room. Imagine that you may have all the money you can carry! Later, when you think of number 5, think of location 5—the front right corner. See the *money* and remember Monroe.

Look at location 6—the right wall—and see a gigantic ad on the wall! You also saw an ad at location 2—the left wall. That's okay. Imagine a gigantic ad covering both the left wall and the right wall—locations 2 and 6! Later, when you think of number 6, think of location 6—the right wall. See the *ad* and remember Adams (the son of the second president).

Look at location 7—the back right corner. Turn and look over your right shoulder at the back right corner. See a gigantic jack (an automobile jack). It reaches from the floor to the ceiling! Later, when you think of number 7, think of location 7—the back right corner. See the *jack* and remember Jackson.

Look at location 8 (the back wall). Imagine that, all of a sudden, a van bursts through the back wall of the room! See it! Hear the crash! Later, when you think of number 8, think of location 8—the back wall. See the *van* and remember Van Buren.

Next, look at location 9 (the floor). See hair growing out of the floor! The entire floor has hair growing out of it! Imagine that you can feel the hair growing up over your ankles, up past your knees—

the hair keeps growing out of the floor! Later, when you think of number 9, think of location 9—the floor. See the *hair* and remember Harrison.

Now that you have mentally stored these nine objects, see if you can recall them forward, backward, and randomly. Cover the Picture and President columns below. Look at each numbered location in sequence and randomly. Recall the picture associated with each numbered location and the president it represents. Uncover to confirm that you are correct.

Room Location	Picture	President
1	washing machine	Washington
2	ad	Adams
3	chef	Jefferson
4	medicine	Madison
5	money	Monroe
6	ad	Adams
7	jack	Jackson
8	van	Van Buren
9	hair	Harrison

How did you do? If you had difficulty remembering the object in any of the locations, it is likely because you did not see or imagine what was in that location as illogically as you should have. When you associate any object with any location, be certain to involve all of your senses, if possible. See it, feel it, hear it, and so forth. Exaggerate the size. Involve yourself in the association (see the object knocking you down, pouring over you, and so on). Be certain you know all nine numbered objects forward, backward, and randomly before continuing.

If you think of the name of a president, you should be able to immediately know his sequential number in office, (such as Jackson is a jack in location 7, so he is the seventh president).

You can quickly discover the power of your own mind through the use of organized memory techniques such as the numbered Cube methodology. Many have told me that they have enjoyed demonstrating the system to their family and friends.

You will use this system often for many different applications. I have used it in corporate, academic, and personal applications to learn and remember:

- Corporate objectives
- Safety procedures
- Schedules and things to do
- An outline of an entire book
- Emergency procedures
- Sequential steps in the operation of equipment
- An airline pilot checkoff list
- The periodic table of the elements in chemistry
- The books of the Bible
- The Ten Commandments
- Speeches and presentations without notes
- How to conduct a business meeting without notes
- Planets in their numbered sequence from the sun
- Zodiac signs
- Grocery lists
- Top ten lists

The use of the Cube methodology is almost limitless. It is fast, easy, dependable, and very practical.

HOW TO SET UP YOUR OWN PERMANENT ROOMS

Although I asked you to use the room in which you are now located for the earlier exercise, I recommend that you use your bedroom to permanently establish a room for the numbers zero through nine because it is likely to be one of your most familiar rooms. Call it your Units Cube or Units room because it includes the single-digit numbers, zero through nine.

You may ask, "How would the Cube method work if there are more than nine things to remember?" Just go (mentally) to another familiar room! If you use your bedroom for the numbers 0 through 9, you may want to use your living room or dining room, for example, for your next room. All that matters is that the room is very familiar to you. You must be able to see the ceiling, the corners, the walls, and the floor, even if you are not physically there.

Your next room is numbered just like your Units room. Start with 0 on the ceiling, then the back left corner (location 1), the left wall (location 2), and continue around the room, ending with the floor (location 9). The only difference is that there is a 1 in front of every number. Therefore, the ceiling is 10, the back left corner is 11, the left wall is 12, and ending with the floor, which is 19. This is called the 10s room because it includes the numbers 10 through 19.

You can easily expand the numbered Cube system to a 20s room (20 through 29), a 30s room (30 through 39), and so on. What makes this system so easy to learn and use is that there is nothing to memorize. If, for example, your kitchen is your 20s room and you need a number 29, just use your 29 location—the floor of your 20s room or the floor of your kitchen. Remember, location 9 is always the floor, so location 49 would be the floor of your 40s room.

How many rooms will you need? For most of your daily needs, two or three rooms are sufficient. If, however, you want to learn anything sequentially numbered that has thirty, fifty, one hundred items or more, such as the presidents of the United States or the periodic table of the elements in chemistry, you will need enough rooms to accommodate the required number. For example, you would need five rooms for the presidents and eleven rooms for the chemical elements.

You might say, "Hold it! I live in a one-room apartment!" That's okay! The rooms need not be in the same house or apartment. They need not even be in the same town.

None of my rooms are in my present residence. They are located miles away where I lived years ago. I can still clearly see there every corner, wall, floor, and ceiling of each room that I use. I can even see the furniture in all of the rooms just as if I had seen the rooms yesterday. That's because I used those rooms for the numbered Cube system when I lived there and I never stopped using them.

Although you may not need more rooms than you have at your present residence, if you do need more rooms, here are a few suggestions:

- A place you used to live (but only if you can clearly see all of the locations within the room or rooms)
- Office(s) where you work
- Your club
- Your church
- A relative's home
- A neighbor's home
- Your garage
- A very familiar restaurant

To practice seeing the numbered room locations, you should prepare a set of flash cards (ten for each room). If you want a memory bank of twenty-nine numbered locations, you will need three rooms (each room ends at the floor with number 9). If you want exactly forty numbered locations, you will need five rooms (but you would use only the ceiling of the fifth room for number 40). Here is an easy way to view it, as well as an example of the various rooms you might use:

first room	0–9	bedroom
next room (10s room)	10–19	living room
next room (20s room)	20–29	den
next room (30s room)	30–39	kitchen
next room (40s room)	40–49	dining room

When you set up your permanent rooms, you should be able to see or imagine every numbered location within every room you are using. It is easier than you may think. For example, you can see your kitchen in your mind—even if you are not in your kitchen right now. You can see your refrigerator in a specific location within your kitchen. You know what color it is. You know if the door opens from the right to the left or from the left to the right. You even know what it looks like inside. But you are not there! That is how the numbered Cube system works. You can see each room location—each corner, every wall, the ceiling, and the floor as well as the furniture—because the room is very familiar to you.

I once gave a memory demonstration while traveling in the Republic of China. I did not use the room in which I was located. I used my familiar rooms half a world away. I remember thinking about that fact at the time. Think about it—even if you were on the moon, you could still see your kitchen and your refrigerator clearly in your mind, from a quarter of a million miles away!

MULTIPLE PROJECTS IN THE SAME ROOMS

One of the most frequently asked questions by those who are just learning the Cube system is, "How can I use my rooms for many different projects without confusing the data?" There are three reasons why this concern should not be a problem:

1. You will be familiar with the subject. By concentrating on that subject, you will find that other objects that you have stored in the same room will not even come to mind.

2. Although a memory system makes it possible to initially store information with relative ease, soon the need for the memory system will disappear and you will know the information you have stored for a given body of knowledge. For example, there are few students of chemistry who know the more than one hundred elements on the periodic table of the elements (name of the element, symbol, atomic number, atomic weight, group, block, and period). Only through a memory system could this information be stored with relative ease and recalled with accuracy and speed. Through frequent use of the memory system, the information becomes permanent knowledge without a conscious use of the system. This system makes it possible to initially store information that may otherwise be very difficult to learn in any reasonable amount of time.

3. If you are working on more than one project at a time, you may use different rooms to eliminate any possible confusion. Also, in the chapters that follow, you will find that there are additional systems that may be used.

HOW TO CHANGE WORDS TO PICTURES

THE AUDIONYM

By seeing how the names of the first nine presidents were changed into soundalike objects, you have already experienced the use of the second of the ten easy steps in my learning system. I call Step 2 the audionym. "Audio" means *sound*. "Nym" means *name*. An audionym is a sound name (a soundalike) for a word you want to remember. It is important to note that audionyms are based on sound, not spelling.

An audionym can be created for any word. Remember, the audionym must be something that sounds like (or at least suggests) the word you want to remember and it must be something you can see. Following are examples of audionyms I have created for a number of subjects:

State	Audionym
Pennsylvania	pencil
Tennessee	tennis (racquet or ball)
Montana	mountain
Delaware	deli
Iowa	eye (soundalike—not spelling)

Country	Audionym
Netherlands	net
Canada	can
Brazil	bracelet
Bulgaria	bull
Bolivia	bowl

Chemical Element	Audionym
hydrogen	hydrant
helium	heel
boron	boar
carbon	car
nitrogen	knight

Planet	Audionym
Mercury	marker
Earth	ear
Jupiter	juice
Neptune	napkin
Pluto	plate

Books of the Bible	Audionym
Genesis	genie
Exodus	exit
Leviticus	leaves
Numbers	numbers
Deuteronomy	detour (sign)

Abstract Word	Audionym
attitude	attic
memory	mummy
organization	organ

Abstract Word	Audionym
motivation	motor
purpose	porpoise

Male Name	Audionym
Dominick	domino
Carl	car
Leigh	leaf
Chen	chin
Ivan	ivy

Female Name	Audionym
Bonnie	bonnet
Shirley	shirt
Juanita	wand
Mollie	mall
Kathryn	cat

Last Name	Audionym
Lennon	linen
Hu	hoop
Fernandez	fern
Fasnacht	faucet
Apostolopolous	a post of lollipops

Part of Speech	Audionym
noun	nun
adverb	ad
conjunction	cone
preposition	pepper
interjection	intersection

Medical Element	Audionym
gastr–	gas truck
dermat–	doormat
cardi–	card
angi–	angel
rhin–	rhinoceros

By reviewing the above words and their suggested audionyms, you will gain an excellent understanding of the audionym technique.

HOW TO CREATE AUDIONYMS

Word	Audionym
Pennsylvania	pencil
Jackson	jack
April	ape

You cannot see a Pennsylvania, a Jackson, or an April, but you can see a pencil, a jack, or an ape. The purpose of the audionym is simply to convert information you want to learn into soundalike objects you can see.

The word *pencil* does not necessarily remind you of the word *Pennsylvania*. However, when you are dealing with the subject States, and *pencil* is the audionym, then Pennsylvania will immediately come to mind. The audionym will be one of your most frequently used memory tools.

Some words suggest obvious audionyms. They immediately suggest an object you can see. If you want to recall China, the country, you could picture china, the dinnerware. Other words become apparent when the sound of the first syllable(s) of the word to remember immediately suggest(s) an object with which you are familiar: *Can*ada, *Pol*and, *Bel*gium, *organ*ization, and so on. Still other words don't immediately suggest anything. Mexico, confidence, and purpose are examples of this. These words require a little more thought to create audionyms. Here are some suggestions:

Word	Audionym
Mexico	mixer
confidence	confetti
purpose	porpoise

When you come to a word for which you need an audionym, say the word fast to see if it brings to mind a soundalike object. Then say it slowly. What object does it sound like to you? Remember, it is how the word *sounds* that counts, not how it is spelled. Remember, also, that the audionym must be something you can see. With just a little practice, audionyms will begin to come to mind quite easily.

Here are more examples of audionyms for last names. Note that they are also the last names of former presidents.

Name	Audionym
Ford	Ford (vehicle)
Van Buren	van
Carter	cart
Eisenhower	eyes
Hayes	hay
Cleveland	cleaver

As you can see in the previous examples, a Ford is already an object you can visualize. The first syllable in the name *Cart*er could suggest *car* or *cart;* I would use *cart* because it is closer to the name Carter. The first syllable of the word *Eis*enhower is not spelled like *eyes,* but it sounds like *eyes.* That makes *eyes* a good audionym for Eisenhower.

CHEMICAL ELEMENTS

Element	Audionym
neon	neon (sign)
lead	lead (pencil)
gold	gold
helium	heel
carbon	car
oxygen	ox
beryllium	barrel
calcium	calculator
fluorine	fluorescent (bulb)

Just by knowing the subject with which you are working, the audionyms will immediately remind you of the word you want to remember. For example, the following audionyms immediately suggest the names of the states they represent:

Audionym	State
mane	Maine
road	Rhode Island
pencil	Pennsylvania
can	Kansas
ark	Arkansas
tacks	Texas
machine	Michigan
flower	Florida

When working with subjects with which you are familiar, such as the states, the word *pencil* should easily remind you of Pennsylvania. But when you are involved with a subject containing unfamiliar words, names, and terms, you will sometimes have to create multiple audionyms for a single word. Algeria might be converted to something such as *owl-cheerleader*.

When creating audionyms, develop the habit of pronouncing the word you want to remember, and then pronounce the audionym. For example, Hayes to hay, Grant to granite, and so forth.

Creating audionyms is the most important technique in my learning system. The more audionyms you create, the easier it becomes.

Remember, audionyms are based on sound, not spelling. They must sound just enough like the word you want to remember to enable you to recall the word later.

It is very important when developing audionyms to know the subject so the audionyms can be kept simple enough to trigger the answer when needed. For example, if you know the subject is major U.S. capital cities, you can probably guess the city represented by each of the following audionyms. Cover the City column. Look at all the audionyms and try to determine the city each of them represents. Uncover to confirm whether you are correct.

MAJOR U.S. CITIES

Audionym	City
den	Denver
sack	Sacramento
Indian	Indianapolis
baton	Baton Rouge
chick	Chicago
detour	Detroit
dollars	Dallas

Audionym	City
buffalo	Buffalo
atlas	Atlanta
sand	San Diego
washing machine	Washington
mill	Milwaukee
salt	Salt Lake City
sail	Salem
medicine	Madison
cleaver	Cleveland
pit	Pittsburgh
witch	Wichita
boss	Boston

How many cities were you able to identify? Had you created the audionyms yourself, identifying them would have been even easier.

It is not necessary to develop audionyms for every syllable of the word you want to recall. In fact, you should not use more than the first syllable if that is enough to trigger the answer and does not lead to confusion with any other item in the subject list.

If the subject is states of the United States, and you need an audionym for Pennsylvania, look at the first syllable in the word *Penn*-syl-van-ia. You see the audionym *pen*. That is probably enough to trigger the answer Pennsylvania. However, *pencil* is also a single object that makes it even easier to recall Pennsylvania, but either one will work—as long as you know the subject is states of the United States.

GUIDELINES FOR CREATING AUDIONYMS

1. Never create an audionym for a word unless you know how to pronounce the word.

2. The audionym must be a soundalike object that you can visualize.

3. You must know the topic or subject on which you are working.

4. You do not have to create an audionym for each syllable in the word you want to remember. The audionym should represent just enough of the beginning of the word to trigger the answer for you. For example, *pen* equals Pennsylvania (or *pencil* equals Pennsylvania). If, in reviewing the material, the information is not clear enough, additional syllables may need audionyms in order to give you the correct answer.

5. If you have difficulty creating an audionym for a word, say the word fast or slow.

6. The audionym does not have to sound exactly like the word you want to remember. Your natural memory and common sense will be an aid.

7. It is not enough for audionyms to just rhyme with the word you want to remember. An audionym should have the same—or very similar—consonant sounds.

The audionym is as basic to my learning system as the alphabet is to the written word. You remember incredibly more of what you see than of what you hear or read. The audionym becomes a picture of the information you want to remember.

Your ability to change the things you hear or read into audionyms will be the key to your success in developing your memory power. Please don't become discouraged if, at first, it takes a while to create audionyms. The more you do it, the easier it becomes.

Step 3

HOW TO REMEMBER BY ASSOCIATION

Step 3 in the learning system is the association of one visual object with another in some illogical way. Using associations to remember things is certainly not new. Ancient scholars used this technique very effectively.

It is interesting to observe how oversimplified some people consider "memory by association." Once I was speaking before an audience of about 600 and had just recalled a 100-digit number given to me in sets of two digits at a time. I had not seen the numbers. I had heard each set only once. After I had successfully recalled the 100 numbers, I heard someone say, "I know how he did it. It's all by association." He was right, of course, but what was I associating with what? To work, the system must be more than just association. It must be simple, effective, fast, and easy. Here are some important things to know about the association technique:

Always start the association with what you will know later. For example, you will know the state for which you want to recall the capital city. You will know the face for which you want to recall the name. You will know the person for whom you want to recall the phone number, and so forth.

Always make the association so illogical that it could never happen in real life. At first, this may take awhile because you may not be accustomed to thinking illogically. In a later chapter, I'll show you how to make the associations illogical enough to work every time.

Every association will involve only two objects at a time, no matter how complex the information is that you want to learn and remember. Nothing you learn will be any more difficult than associating two objects together in an illogical way just like you did when you saw the nine objects in the Cube for the first nine presidents.

HOW TO CREATE POWERFUL ASSOCIATIONS

It is difficult to convince people that a well-developed memory is not something a person is born with. Memory training is no different than any other learned skill. There are certain procedures to follow and a degree of mental dexterity that comes with practice. With the exception of hypnosis and the electronic or chemical stimulation of brain cells, there are only three ways we remember:

1. **Repetition.** This has always been the most common method of learning because it is the only method with which most people are familiar. Organized memory techniques are not widely known. Learning by repetition is time-consuming and inefficient. Information learned by repetition must be continually repeated in order to be retained. In fact, as soon

as repetition stops, forgetting starts. No matter what learning style is used (visual, auditory, kinesthetic, and so on), repetition is the least efficient method of learning. Isn't it ironic that the least efficient method of learning is the most predominant method of teaching throughout our formal education?

2. **Impression.** This method works, but is the least practical because we do not get to choose what we will recall through impression. Memory by impression occurs when we encounter a traumatic experience—such as something that leaves such an impact or impression upon our minds that we could not forget it even if we tried.

3. **Association.** This involves illogically associating what you want to remember with something you already know. This is, without question, far superior to any other method for remembering. First, it capitalizes on your natural ability to remember what you see. Secondly, it is easier to remember things that are illogical, exaggerated in size or quantity, or out-of-proportion.

The printed words we read and the spoken words we hear usually have no pictures associated with them as they arrive at the point of our senses. I suspect that those who have what we refer to as good natural memories are people who subconsciously see pictures for spoken or printed words. Some image undoubtedly flashes in their minds that allows them to retain information better than the average person. Most of us, however, are not in that category, so we must train ourselves to organize the information we want to remember by using memory systems. These allow us to see information we hear and read and to lock it into our memories.

The technique of association, when properly organized, requires two necessary elements: "what you already know" and "what you want to remember." For example, when meeting a person for the first time, there are two basic elements to be associated: the name and the face. At some future time, when you want to recall the name, you will already know the person's face.

Have you ever heard someone say, "I remember your face, but I'm sorry, I just can't recall your name." Sure you have! But, have you ever heard anyone say, "Hi, Joe," or "Hi, Sally, I remember your name but I just cannot recall your face"? No! That just doesn't happen! You see the face and you remember it because you remember what you see. You hear the name and you forget it because you forget what you hear.

Every association must begin with what you know. For example, if you want to remember your friend Joe's telephone number, you would not associate Joe with the phone number. You would associate the phone number with Joe. In this case, Joe is what you know (because you will know that it is Joe whom you want to call). The phone number is what you want to remember. You would never think, "This is the number I want to call. Whose number is it?" Instead, you would think, "I want to call Joe, what is his number?"

To make an effective association of any two objects, you must establish what you will know when you need to recall it, then associate what you want to remember with what you will know. Through the power of association, you will learn to systematically store data in your mind and retrieve it with incredible accuracy. For the moment, it is important that you remember to begin every association with a known factor (what you are certain you will know when it is time to recall the information being mentally stored).

You may have frequently heard the phrase "memory by association." To be effective, an association must be illogical. The more illogical the association, the easier it will be to remember. Which one of the following associations would you most easily remember if you were to see it in real life?

Example 1	**Example 2**	**Example 3**
Logical	Illogical	Illogical
	(but possible)	(impossible)

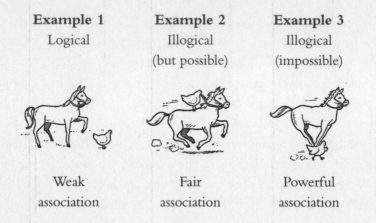

Weak	Fair	Powerful
association	association	association

In the first example, the chicken and horse were associated in a logical way. While this may work occasionally, it is too common and would not likely be retained for too long. In the second example, the association is illogical and could be retained for a longer period of time. Although this example is illogical, it is possible that such an event could occur. The third example shows an association so illogical that it could never happen! For this reason, it is a very powerful and effective association.

Any two items can be associated with each other. Again, every association you make with my learning system will involve only two objects at a time. The objects, themselves, do not have to be illogical. It is how the objects are mentally associated that makes the mental image illogical.

It is critical, in any association, to know which is the known object (what you will know when it is time to recall what you want to remember). The other object is the information you want to remember.

GUIDELINES FOR CREATING ASSOCIATIONS

1. Identify the "known" (what you will know at the time you want to recall the information) and change it to an audionym (a soundalike you can see). If the known is in the numbered Cube or is a physical location, there is no need to create an audionym because you can already see it.

2. Identify the information you want to remember and change it to an audionym.

3. Visualize the known audionym in its normal location (or a physical location in its normal place).

4. Associate the information you want to remember with the *known* audionym or location.

5. Be certain when making your association that it is so unusual, ridiculous, amusing, illogical, or out-of-proportion that it could never happen in real life.

6. Multiply the data audionym. Your association can usually be strengthened by visualizing the data audionym multiplied by hundreds or even millions.

7. Use all of your senses, if necessary, to strengthen your association. Immerse yourself in the illogical association. *See* it! *Hear* it! *Feel* it! *Smell* it! *Taste* it!

8. The more action you can incorporate into your association, the easier it will be to remember.

9. Personal involvement. Involve yourself, when possible, in your associations. When it is you who is involved, it will make more of an impression on your mind.

10. As a general rule, if the association is possible in real life, it is not illogical enough.

The known audionym or physical location will always be clear to you. In the following examples, they appear in **bold** type:

1. When you see a **face** and want to remember the name.

2. When you want to call a **person** or **place** and need the number.

3. When you need your **car keys** or **glasses,** or **another item,** and wonder where you put them.

4. When you think of a **state** and wish to remember its capital city.

5. When you think of a **book title** and wish to remember its author.

6. When you think of a **food** and want to know its calories.

7. When you think of a **motion picture** and want to recall the actors and actresses.

The guidelines for creating illogical associations are simple, but you must practice and apply these rules until they become "a way of life." Association is the most basic and surely one of the most important of all memory techniques. You will use the association technique in every memory system I teach you in this book.

It is necessary to know how the association technique works before you apply it to specific information. It's sort of like learning the individual notes on the musical scale before applying the notes to a specific song.

MORE PRACTICAL APPLICATIONS USING ASSOCIATION

So far, you have learned three memory techniques: the numbered Cube, the audionym, and association. The only reason to create audionyms is to change what you hear and read into things you can see. Associations are created in order to rapidly learn and easily recall information. Here are some practical applications for the association technique:

Data	Known
artist of a	painting
date of an	event
definition of a	word
price of an	item
combination to a	lock
meaning of a	foreign word
formula for a	math problem
symbol for a	chemical element
dates of the	zodiac signs
area code for a	city
definition of a	part of speech
code for an	airport
number of an	airline flight
departure time of	transportation

Some of my students have actually made a hobby of remembering notable achievements and statistics. This is another natural application of the association technique. Again, it is necessary to have a known and the information you want to remember:

Information	Known
highest	waterfall
longest	river
tallest	building
most	home runs
fastest	runners
largest	planet
youngest	president

Soon you will find limitless practical applications for this powerful association technique.

PROJECT INFORMATION VS. RANDOM INFORMATION

I place everything I want to remember into just two categories: project information and random information. Some examples of project information are learning a world language, the periodic table of elements, the presidents and their terms of office, the states and capitals, medical terminology, and so on. With these types of projects, you have time to analyze what you want to remember.

Some examples of random information are remembering a person's name, a phone number, an address, the author of a book, directions, or cards that are played in a card game. With these types of information, you have to create a way to remember the information "on the spot." There is no time to analyze it.

Following are some examples of the association technique used in project information. I recognize that you may have no interest in the content of the information. Again, what is important is not the content, but the methodology. Simply by "seeing how it is done" for various subjects, you will learn how to use the system on your own for unlimited applications.

ASSOCIATION APPLIED TO MEDICAL TERMINOLOGY

The most successful of my applied learning systems so far is the course on medical terminology. It was first published in 1974 and is the world's first commercially successful applied memory system. More than 2.5 million individuals have completed the course in more than 10,000 academic and business institutions worldwide.

A medical term is made up of elements or word parts called roots, prefixes, and suffixes. The root element is always the subject or main topic of the medical term—frequently a body part. The prefix element appears at the beginning of a medical term and changes, in some manner, the meaning of the medical term or makes it more specific. The suffix element appears at the end of a medical term (after the root element), and frequently describes a condition of a body part or an action to a body part. A medical term may include more than one root element.

The course teaches 350 elements (prefixes, roots, and suffixes) that can be combined into more than 11,000 complex medical terms. Here are a few examples and a description of how the system works:

Medical Element	Audionym
gastr-	gas truck
cardi-	cards
blephar-	blue fur

Medical Element	Audionym
derma-	doormat
aden-	a den
–itis	"I test" (a teacher saying, "I test my students!")

ASSOCIATIONS

gastr- See a **gas truck** with a **stomach** for a tank! (**gastr-** means **stomach**)

cardi- See people playing **cards** with real **hearts!** (**cardi-** means **heart**)

blephar- See a lady wearing a **blue fur** (artificial, of course). It has **eyelids** all over it! (**blephar-** means **eyelid**)

derma- See a **doormat** covered with real **skin** (**derma-** means **skin**)

aden- See a **den** with **glands** covering the walls! (**aden-** means **gland**)

-itis See a teacher saying "**I test**" **in flames!** (**-itis** means **inflammation**)

The first five elements are root elements and represent body parts. The element -itis is a suffix meaning *inflammation*. When these elements are combined to form medical terms, they are read and interpreted from the right to the left. For example:

gastritis (gastr/itis)	inflammation of the stomach
carditis (card/itis)	inflammation of the heart
blepharitis (blephar/itis)	inflammation of the eyelid
dermatitis (derma/t/itis)	inflammation of the skin
gastroadenitis (gastr/o/aden/itis)	inflammation of the glands of the stomach
blepharadenitis (belphar/aden/itis)	inflammation of the glands of the eyelid

You would not need a memory system to learn just these few medical elements and terms, but, if you want or need to know thousands of complex medical terms, there is no faster way to learn and remember them than to use an organized memory system. In less than fourteen hours individuals are able to interpret and define more than 11,000 complex medical terms. That is more of the language of medicine than most physicians know.

The medical terminology course was initially designed for

the insurance industry. As a former vice-president of Pennsylvania Blue Shield, I recognized the need for claims examiners to know the language of medicine. Most claims examiners at insurance companies are required to have a much more extensive knowledge of medical terms than most physicians in order to properly adjudicate medical claims received from physicians of all specialties.

The medical terminology course is used by every major health insurance company in America. It has been used by more than 2.5 million students and employees in more than 10,000 organizations such as hospitals, academic institutions, the military, and many state and federal government agencies.

LATIN AND GREEK FOR ENGLISH VOCABULARY

Most tests, whether they are designed to measure academic achievement in our schooling, or to demonstrate verbal aptitude for employment, include a section on vocabulary. The value of a powerful vocabulary is inestimable. Your word power will play a major role in your academic, business, professional, and social success. It is the key to self-confidence in speaking, writing, and reading comprehension.

One of the most practical and rewarding applications of my learning system is in building a powerful vocabulary. Just as knowing several hundred medical elements would enable you to interpret and define more than 11,000 medical terms, knowing several hundred Latin and Greek elements or word parts would enable you to increase your English vocabulary by tens of thousands of words!

Following are five examples of Latin and Greek elements (word parts) used in English vocabulary. You will be amazed at how quickly you will learn them and how easily you will remember them with an organized learning system.

Element	Audionym	Association	Meaning
-archy	ark	ruler (for measuring)	ruler (person)

See an **ark** with a gigantic **ruler** (for measuring) in it! The **ruler** (for measuring) will help you remember **ruler** (one who rules or governs), the meaning of **archy**.

Examples: anarchy, patriarchy, matriarchy, monarchy, hierarchy, oligarchy.

Element	Audionym	Association	Meaning
culp-	cup	bloom	blame

See a **cup** filled with a gigantic **bloom** of flowers! **Bloom** will help you remember **blame,** the meaning of **culp.**

Examples: culpable, culprit, exculpate, inculpable, culpa.

Element	Audionym	Association	Meaning
chron-	crayon	timer (egg timer)	time

See a **crayon** with a **timer** (egg timer) tied around it! **Timer** will help you remember **time,** the meaning of **chron.**

Examples: chronic, anachronistic, synchronize, chronicle, chronology, chronological, chronometer, chronometric.

Element	Audionym	Association	Meaning
-escent	a cent	bee combing	becoming

See **a cent** with a **bee combing** its hair on it! **Bee combing** will help you remember **becoming,** the meaning of **-escent.**

Examples: adolescent, incandescent, acquiescent, convalescent, iridescent, effervescent, obsolescent, opalescent.

Element	Audionym	Association	Meaning
ben-	bench	gold	good

See a **bench** made of **gold**! **Gold** will help you remember **good,** the meaning of **ben.**

Examples: beneficial, benevolent, beneficiary, benign, benefit, benefactor, benediction, bencfice, benefactress, benefaction, benefic, beneficence.

REVIEW

Element	Audionym	Association	Meaning
-archy	ark	ruler (for measuring)	ruler (person)
culp-	cup	bloom	blame
chron-	crayon	timer (for measuring)	time
-escent	a cent	bee combing	becoming
ben-	bench	gold	good

The five elements (word parts) you have just learned were used in forty-one words as examples. There are many more. Can you imagine how rapidly you could develop your English vocabulary if you combine these elements with others? Not only would you have a better understanding of words you have seen or heard (and may not have fully understood), but you would also have a good idea of the meanings of many thousands of words you have never even seen or heard. This demonstrates the importance of learning Latin and Greek word prefixes, roots, and suffixes. It also makes the study of world languages much easier because the vocabulary of multiple languages can often be traced to the same Latin or Greek prefixes, roots, or suffixes.

Anyone desiring to be a better communicator should recognize the importance of a powerful vocabulary. You are frequently judged by the words you use. Now there is a way to dramatically increase your vocabulary, faster and easier than you have ever dreamed possible.

ASSOCIATION APPLIED TO
ENGLISH VOCABULARY

You can now build your English vocabulary at the amazing rate of one new word per minute! Following are five examples of English words and how to remember them. This strategy works just like the application to Latin and Greek, except that it is applied to complete English words instead of word parts.

English	Audionym	Association	Meaning
abstract	Abe's tractor	theater	theoretical

See **Abe's tractor** with a **theater** on it! **Theater** will help you remember **theoretical,** the meaning of **abstract.**

English	Audionym	Association	Meaning
spurious	spur	falls	false (fake)

See a **spur** with a water **falls** pouring out of it! **Falls** will help you remember, **false,** the meaning of **spurious.**

English	Audionym	Association	Meaning
manifest	man in a vest	visor	visible

See a **man in a vest.** The **vest** has a gigantic **visor** on it! **Visor** will help you remember **visible,** the meaning of **manifest.**

English	Audionym	Association	Meaning
fetter	feather	restaurant	restrain

See a **feather** with a **restaurant** on it! **Restaurant** will help you remember **restrain,** the meaning of **fetter.**

English	Audionym	Association	Meaning
petulant	pet ant	crank	cranky (rude)

See a **pet ant** holding a **crank**! **Crank** will help you remember **cranky,** the meaning of **petulant.**

REVIEW

English	Audionym	Association	Meaning
abstract	Abe's tractor	theater	theoretical
spurious	spur	falls	false (fake)
manifest	man in a vest	visor	visible
fetter	feather	restaurant	restrain
petulant	pet ant	crank	cranky (rude)

WORLD LANGUAGE VOCABULARY: LEARN ONE NEW SPANISH WORD PER MINUTE!

Start with what you know—English. If the English word is a noun, you can already see it. If it is not a noun, change it to an audionym. Then, change the meaning into an audionym. Associate the two audionyms.

apple — See an **apple** with a **man in a sauna** inside it! **Man in a sauna** will help you remember *manzana* (mahn-SAH-nah), the Spanish word for **apple**.

bread — See (imagine) **bread** with a **pan** bursting out of it! **Pan** will help you remember *pan* (pronounced PAHN), the Spanish word for **bread**.

potato — See a **potato** with a **papa** in it! **Papa** will help you remember *papa* (PAH-pah), the Spanish word for **potato**.

butter — See **butter** with a **man** holding **two keys** standing in it! **Man-two keys** will help you remember *mantequilla* (pronounced mahn-teh-KEE-yah), the Spanish word for **butter**.

soup — See **soup** with **soap** in it! **Soap** will help you remember *sopa* (pronounced SOH-pah), the Spanish word for **soup**.

REVIEW

English	Audionym	Association	Spanish
apple	apple	man in a sauna	manzana
bread	bread	pan	pan
potato	potato	papa	papa
butter	butter	man/two keys	mantequilla
soup	soup	soap	sopa

Step 4

THE LINK SYSTEM

Step 4 in the learning system, called the Link system, will be by far the easiest to learn and apply because it is simply a repeat of the association technique. In the association technique, what you want to learn is associated with something you already know.

In the Link system, there are still only two things to be associated. The only difference is that the information you wanted to learn in the first association becomes the information you already know for the next association (the known). In the following example, start with the sun (something you already know and can see). Five audionyms, representing the first five planets, will be linked together and are presented in their sequence from the sun.

Known	Association	Audionym	Planet
Sun	See the **sun** with a gigantic **marker** bursting out of it!	**marker**	Mercury
marker	See the **marker** with a **V-neck sweater** hanging on it!	V-neck sweater	Venus

Known	Association	Audionym	Planet
V neck Sweater	See the **V-neck sweater** with a gigantic **ear** on it!	**ear**	Earth
ear	See the **ear** with a huge **marshmallow** in it!	**marshmallow**	Mars
marshmallow	See the **marshmallow** with **juice** pouring out of it!	**juice**	Jupiter

How to Recall the Linked Audionyms

Think of the sun and recall the **marker** (Mercury)
Think of the **marker** and recall the **V-neck sweater** (Venus)
Think of the **V-neck sweater** and recall the **ear** (Earth)
Think of the **ear** and recall the **marshmallow** (Mars)
Think of the **marshmallow** and recall the **juice** (Jupiter)

Now think of just these audionyms: sun, marker, V-neck sweater, ear, marshmallow, and juice. By remembering this simple link, starting with what you already know (the sun) it is easy to remember the first five planets in their sequence from the sun.

To create this link, I looked at the names of the first five planets and changed each of them into an audionym. Then, I started with the sun (the known) and linked the audionyms one at a time by creating five associations.

Sun/Planets	Audionym
Sun	Sun (what you already know)
Mercury	marker
Venus	V-neck sweater
Earth	ear
Mars	marshmallow
Jupiter	juice

I used the planets just as an example of how easy it is to link objects together with each new bit of information becoming the known for the next link. The Link system is a very important part of the learning system. You will use it often in combination with the other techniques for many practical applications.

Suggested audionyms for the remaining four planets in our solar system (in their sequence from the sun) are:

Planet	Audionym
Saturn	sac or sap
Uranus	urn or unicorn
Neptune	napkin
Pluto	plate

For practice, link the audionyms for the remaining four planets.

Later, I'll show you some examples of the amazing power of your mind when you combine several of the techniques at once.

Step 5

HOW TO REMEMBER NUMBERS

THE NUMBER CODE

According to psychologists, the most difficult things to remember in our daily lives are numbers. This is because numbers are abstract symbols for which we have no immediate visual images. Multiple-digit numbers further complicate the problem.

The average individual can recall no more than a seven-digit number after having heard it one time. I suppose this may have something to do with the fact that most local telephone numbers are only seven digits, and, therefore, that is about the longest number most people need to remember on a daily basis.

Since you remember incredibly well the things you see, we'll change abstract numerical symbols into tangible visual pictures. This is achieved by first converting numbers into consonant letters of the alphabet, then into words.

Virtually every memory course uses the same system for remembering numbers. Without elaborating on the history of memory systems, I will simply tell you that this number-alphabetic character technique has been in use in various forms for hundreds of years. It is amazing to me, however, that virtually no one has used it in practical applications. From this point on, I will refer to this technique only as the Number Code. We'll begin with the code in its simplest form, then expand it later.

There are only ten digits used as the basis for our numbering system (0 through 9). Only the consonant sounds from the alphabet are used in the code. The vowels (a, e, i, o, u) and the half-vowels (h, w, y) have no number value. Notice that if we rearrange the sequence of the half-vowels (h, w, y) we can create the word *why*. This will make them easier to remember.

Here is the Number Code:

0 = s	5 = l
1 = t	6 = ch
2 = n	7 = c (hard c, as in "coat") or k
3 = m	8 = f
4 = r	9 = p

You can use the Cube method to quickly learn and easily remember the Number Code. Just select a familiar room that you will call your Number Code room. Imagine yourself facing the front wall of your Number Code room.

I am going to ask you to see an object at each of the ten numbered locations in the Cube (zero through nine). Each object will be something people eat or drink. For the even numbers, 0, 2, 4, 6, and 8 (ceiling, left wall, front wall, right wall, and back wall), I'll give you foods people eat. For the odd numbers, 1, 3, 5, 7, and 9 (back left corner, front left corner, front right corner, back right corner, and the floor), I'll give you beverages people drink. The first sound of each food or beverage is the sound of the code for its respective number.

0 = S

To learn and remember that the code for 0 is s, see spaghetti hanging all over the ceiling! The first sound in the word *spaghetti,* is s. The code for 0 is s.

1 = T

To remember that the code for 1 is t, see a gigantic cup of tea at location 1, the back left corner. The first sound in the word *tea,* is t. The code for 1 is t.

2 = N

To remember that the code for 2 is n, see noodles all over the left wall (location 2). The first sound in the word *noodles,* is n. The code for 2 is n.

3 = M

To remember that the code for 3 is m, see a gigantic carton of milk at location 3, the front left corner. The first sound in the word *milk,* is m. The code for 3 is m.

4 = R

To remember that the code for 4 is r, see a gigantic mound of rice at the front wall (location 4). The first sound in the word *rice,* is r. The code for 4 is r.

5 = L

To remember that the code for 5 is l, see a gigantic pitcher of lemonade at location 5, the front right corner. The first sound in the word *lemonade,* is l. The code for 5 is l.

6 = CH

To remember that the code for 6 is ch, see a gigantic wedge of cheese at the right wall (location 6). The first sound in the word *cheese,* is ch. The code for 6 is ch.

7 = Hard C or K

To remember that the code for 7 is c (as in *coffee*), see a gigantic cup of coffee at location 7, the back right corner. The first sound in the word *coffee,* is c. The code for 7 is c.

8 = F

To remember that the code for 8 is f, see gigantic fruit at the back wall (location 8). The first sound in the word *fruit,* is f. The code for 6 is f.

9 = P

To remember that the code for 9 is p, see a gigantic bowl of punch at location 9, the floor. The first sound in the word *punch,* is p. The code for 9 is p.

Review

0	spaghetti	s
1	tea	t
2	noodles	n
3	milk	m
4	rice	r
5	lemonade	l
6	cheese	ch
7	coffee	c (or k)
8	fruit	f
9	punch	p

Please note that in practical applications, it is best to develop the habit of always pronouncing the sound, rather than the name of the consonant.

Cover the Code column. Look at each number and recall the code. Uncover to check. Then, cover the Number column. Look at each code and recall the number. Uncover to check.

Number	Code
3	m
5	l
9	p
0	s
6	ch
8	f
1	t
2	n
7	c, k
4	r

You should practice this exercise until you can look at any number and immediately know its corresponding sound. Conversely, you should be able to look at any letter, say its sound, and know its corresponding number.

Please do not continue until you have mastered the above code.

Numbers can be changed to pictures (Code Words) using the Number Code. Let's start with number 32. You already know that 3 is m and 2 is n. So think of the number 32 like this:

32

m–n

Remember, the vowels (a, e, i, o, u) and the letters w, h, y have no number value. Therefore, you can use as many vowels in a Code Word as you wish, but make sure not to use any more consonants than are represented by the number.

The number 32 could be changed to numerous Code Words:

32	32	32	32	32
mane	mine	moon	money	minnow

Please note that double consonants always have a single sound because you hear only one sound in a double consonant. In changing numbers into Code Words, it is not how a word is spelled but how it sounds that counts.

It is important that the Code Word be an object. Just as an audionym must be an object you can see, the Code Word (the word you create from a number) must be a tangible object.

Here are more examples:

45	45	45	45	45
rail	reel	rule	rally	roll

34	34	34	34
mare	mower	hammer	mayor

As you can see, there are many Code Words you could choose for a number. The rules for converting numbers into Code Words are:

1. Numbers can be converted only to their assigned consonant sounds. The following letters have no number value:

   a, e, i, o, u
   h, w, y (as a memory aid, rearrange to "w, h, y")
   any silent consonant

2. The Code Words must represent something tangible.
3. Double consonants have a single consonant sound. Therefore, double consonants represent a single number.
4. It is how the Code Word sounds and not how it is spelled that counts.
5. Any number may be converted into more than one Code Word, but a Code Word can be converted only to a specific number.

For example, the number 35 can be converted to any of the following Code Words:

mail	mule
meal	mile
mole	male
mill	mall

All of these Code Words can be converted *only* to the number 35:

mail	mule
meal	mile
mole	male
mill	mall

The Code Word **n**ail can be converted only to 25.
The Code Word **r**ain can be converted only to 42.
The Code Word **t**ail can be converted only to 15.
The Code Word **t**ire can be converted only to 14.

Convert the following words to two-digit numbers (the answers follow):

ram	lion	net	moon	tin
mule	root	sail	mat	mare
reel	lure	mayor	army	worm
heart	lamb	knot	twine	mane

Answers:

43	52	21	32	12
35	41	05	31	34
45	54	34	43	43
41	53	21	12	32

Notice how the following three-digit numbers can be converted to multiple Code Words. You will use three-digit numbers often for telephone number prefixes, area codes, and page numbers.

314	141	210	351
motor	**trout**	**nuts**	**malt**
meter	**torte**	**gnats**	**mallet**
miter	**treat**	**ants**	**omelet**

Cover the answers that follow. Convert the following words to three-digit numbers. Uncover to check your answers.

steam	**train**	**tutor**
mist	**rust**	**tools**
nylon	**lariat**	**sailor**
missile	**toast**	**memory**
snail	**notary**	**mitten**

Answers:

013	142	114
301	401	150
252	541	054
305	101	334
025	214	312

Cover the answers that follow. Change the following two-digit numbers to Code Words: I will give you one Code Word. Try to think of at least one more.

Any word will be correct if the two consonant sounds represent the two numbers and if you can see the object. (Some suggested words appear below.)

43 ream	35 mall	71 coat
21 note	52 loan	82 fan
41 root	14 tower	99 pipe
45 reel	32 mine	62 chain
53 lime	31 moat	79 cap

Here are some suggested words:

43	ream, ram, rum, room, arm, rhyme, rim
21	note, net, knight, newt, knot, nut, gnat
41	root, rate, rot, rut, heart, rat, wart
45	reel, roll, rally, rail, rule
53	lime, loom, elm, helm
35	mall, mail, mule, mile, mill, meal
52	loan, line, lion, lane, loin
14	tower, tire, tear, tour, tree
32	mine, moon, money, mane, men, man

31	moat, meat, mat, mitt, mutt, mate
71	coat, cat, cot, coyote
82	fan, fin, fawn, fine
99	pipe, Pope, pop, pup, pap, peep
62	chain, chin
79	cap, cup, coop, cop, cape

Cover the answers that follow. Change the following three-digit numbers to Code Words. I will give you one Code Word. Try to think of at least one more.

514	**lighter**
314	**matter**
012	**stein**
321	**minuet**

Some suggested answers:

514	lighter, letter, liter, looter, lottery
314	matter, meter, miter, motor
012	stein, stone, stain
321	minuet, minute, mint

76	85	68	92	69	74	96
couch	file	chief	pin	chip	car	peach
coach	fly	chef	pawn	chop	core	pouch

Although you have now learned the Number Code for zero through nine, the versatility of this code can be tremendously expanded by adding like-consonant sounds to those sounds you already know.

Some consonant sounds, or combinations of them, are similar and can, therefore, be assigned to the same number. Notice how your mouth, lips, teeth, and tongue are framed the same way to say p or b, t or d, s or c (as in celery), etc. Following is the expanded Number Code:

0　S (as in **s**ew, **s**ea, **s**aw)
　　C (as in **c**elery, **c**ymbal, when C sounds like S)
　　Z (as in **z**oo, **z**ebra, **z**odiac)
1　T (as in **t**oe, **t**ea, **t**ie)
　　D (as in **d**oe, **d**ew, **d**ye)
　　TH (as in **th**eater, **th**istle, **th**imble)
2　N (as in **n**oon, **n**ame, **n**ote)
3　M (as in **m**ow, **m**a, **m**oon)
4　R (as in **r**ow, **r**ye, **r**ain)
5　L (as in **l**ow, **l**aw, **l**ane)
6　CH (as in **ch**eese, **ch**ow, **ch**amp)
　　SH (as in **sh**oe, **sh**ow, **sh**ower)
　　G (soft, as in **g**em, **g**in, **g**ym)
　　J (as in **j**aw, **j**am, **j**ar)
7　C (hard, as in **c**ow, **c**at, **c**an)
　　K (as in **k**ite, **k**it, **k**id)
　　G (hard, as in **g**oat, **g**ame, **g**amble)
　　Q (as in **q**ueen, **q**uake, **q**uack)
8　F (as in **f**oe, **f**an, **f**ur)
　　V (as in **v**ine, **v**ase, **v**ice)
　　PH (as in **ph**one, **ph**oto)
9　P (as in **p**ie, **p**ea, **p**ew)
　　B (as in **b**ow, **b**ee, **b**ay)

REVIEW

```
0  =  S, C (soft), Z
1  =  T, D, TH
2  =  N
3  =  M
4  =  R
5  =  L
6  =  CH, SH, G (soft), J
7* =  C (hard), K, G (hard), Q
8  =  F, V, PH
9  =  P, B
```

*Note: Also CK, since it has a hard C or K sound. For example, the CK in so**ck**, ne**ck**, ro**ck**, che**ck**, and so on.

Study the Code until you can look at any number and know its corresponding sound(s) or any sound and know its corresponding number. You will use this Number Code many times in this book. More important, once you have mastered it, you are likely to use it every day for the rest of your life.

PRACTICAL APPLICATIONS OF THE NUMBER CODE:
TELEPHONE AREA CODES

There are thousands of applications of the Number Code. One very practical and timesaving use of this technique is for remembering telephone numbers. In fact, with the Number Code, it is much faster and easier to remember telephone numbers than to look them up!

Here is an example of how the Number Code can be applied to the area codes for cities, while recognizing that some cities have multiple codes:

City	Area Code
Chicago	312
Atlanta	404
Indianapolis	317
Baton Rouge	504
Dallas	214
Milwaukee	414
Lincoln	402
Erie	814
Des Moines	515
Columbus	614

How to remember area codes for each of the following cities (there are multiple codes in most major cities):

City	Audionym	Code Word	Area Code
Chicago	chick	mitten	312

See a **chick (Chicago)** wearing a **mitten (312)** (chick-mitten).

City	Audionym	Code Word	Area Code
Atlanta	Atlas	razor	404

See an **atlas (Atlanta)** with a **razor (404)** stuck through it (atlas-razor).

City	Audionym	Code Word	Area Code
Indianapolis	Indian	medic	317

See an **Indian (Indianapolis)** as a **medic (317)** (Indian-medic).

City	Audionym	Code Word	Area Code
Baton Rouge	baton	laser	504

See a **baton (Baton Rouge)** with a **laser (504)** shining out of it (baton–laser).

City	Audionym	Code Word	Area Code
Dallas	dollars	hunter	214

See **dollars (Dallas)** with a **hunter (214)** on them (dollars-hunter).

City	Audionym	Code Word	Area Code
Milwaukee	mill	radar	414

See a **mill (Milwaukee)** with a **radar (414)** screen on it (mill-radar).

City	Audionym	Code Word	Area Code
Lincoln	Lincoln	raisin	402

See Abe **Lincoln (Lincoln)** with a huge **raisin (402)** in his hat (Lincoln-raisin).

City	Audionym	Code Word	Area Code
Erie	ear	feather	814

See an **ear (Erie)** with a **feather (814)** stuck in it (ear-feather).

City	Audionym	Code Word	Area Code
Des Moines	domino	ladle	515

See a **domino (Des Moines)** with a **ladle (515)** stuck through it (domino-ladle).

City	Audionym	Code Word	Area Code
Columbus	column	cheddar	614

See a **column (Columbus)** made of **cheddar (614)** cheese (column-cheddar).

Later, when you want to remember the area code for these or other cities:

1. Think of the audionym for the city.
2. See the object (Code Word) you associated with it.
3. Change the Code Word to its three-digit area code.

REVIEW

City	Audionym	Association	Area Code
Chicago	chick	**mitten**	312
Atlanta	Atlas	**razor**	404
Indianapolis	Indian	**medic**	317
Baton Rouge	baton	**laser**	504
Dallas	dollars	**hunter**	214
Milwaukee	mill	**radar**	414
Lincoln	Lincoln	**raisin**	402
Erie	ear	**feather**	814
Des Moines	domino	**ladle**	515
Columbus	column	**cheddar**	614

HOW TO REMEMBER TELEPHONE NUMBERS

The ideal way to remember a phone number is to change the three-digit prefix into a single Code Word and associate it with a Code Word for the four-digit suffix. For example, 741-9214 could be converted to **cart-painter**. Visualize a **cart** with a **painter** in it.

Wouldn't it be nice if every telephone number could be changed into Code Words by finding a single word for both the three-digit prefix and the four-digit suffix? Unfortunately, it usually doesn't work that way. Often, however, it is possible to change the prefix to a single Code Word. For example:

432-	532-	742-	357-	471-
Roman-	**lemon-**	**corn-**	**milk-**	**rocket-**

Many times it is necessary to scan the entire seven-digit number in order to find the right combination because the Code Word(s) may not be immediately obvious.

The number 750-1390 is listed below six times, with six different sets of Code Words. There are many more Code Words that could be used. The important thing is that the Code Words need not be related at all—just associated together by forming a link of the objects they represent.

750-1390	750-1390	750-1390
coals-dome bus	**coal-stamps**	**closet-mops**

750-1390	750-1390	750-1390
clothes-dime pies	**glass-dome bus**	**clay-stumps**

Learning telephone numbers is a two-step process:

1. Create Code Words for the telephone numbers.
2. Associate the phone number with the person or place to which the number belongs.

Remembering phone numbers in your local area is often much easier. For example, in some small towns there is only one prefix. In this case, you need a memory system only for the last four digits (-xxxx).

In those areas where the first two digits of the prefix are the same, as in 243-xxxx and 249-xxxx, apply the Number Code only to the last digit of the prefix and to the four-digit suffix (x-xxx).

It is unnecessary and inefficient to apply a memory system to anything you already know through your natural memory or common sense!

Soon you will learn a Code Word for every two-digit number from 00 through 99. Each Code Word will be the word you always use for a particular two-digit number, and, therefore, will be called the Key Word. After you know the Key Words for every two-digit number, learning telephone numbers will be a snap!

Obviously, the ideal approach to learning a telephone number is to use only one Code Word, but this opportunity seldom occurs.

If you ever have difficulty creating a Code Word for a four-digit number, you will always be able to comfortably rely on the Key Word system taught in the next chapter.

In remembering telephone numbers, there are really only two items involved: a name (or place) and a number. The name (or place) must be changed into an audionym (or object) and the number must be changed into Code Words.

If the number to remember is that of a friend, acquaintance, or a place with which you are familiar, you already have a starting point. If you are learning a list of phone numbers for persons or places with which you are not familiar, you must have a visual image of either the person or the place. Remembering telephone numbers is really just an association and link technique: you associate the phone number (its code) with the person or place to whom it belongs.

Let's suggest that the telephone number for your bank is 352-5200.

1. See the bank in your mind's eye.
2. Change the number (352-5200) into Code Words: for example, **melon-lion-see**saw.

3. Associate the phone number—**me**l**o**n-**l**i**o**n-**s**eesaw—with the bank.

For example, visualize the bank as a gigantic **melon**. As you look at the **melon** a **lion** leaps out with a **seesaw** in its mouth! With a clear visual image of the bank in your mind, think, bank, see melon-lion-seesaw, and remember 352-5200.

Now try the system for a phone number you would like to learn. Pick one that you call on occasion, but that you do not know—your bank, the pizza place, the post office, and so on.

1. You already have a visual image of the person or place.

2. Change the phone number into Code Words. Link them together, starting with the first Code Word.

3. Associate the first Code Word with the person or place.

The remaining link of Code Words will fall into place.

When learning telephone numbers, it is a common error to recall the Code Words (objects) out of order. Because there are so few objects, you can see them all at once and, therefore, tend to disregard the sequence.

When recalling the objects (Code Words) for a telephone number, it is not good enough just to see all of the objects. You must see them in their proper sequence! In the previous example, you may remember all three objects—the Code Words—we associated with the bank: melon-seesaw-lion.

You are correct if you remember these as the three objects, but you are incorrect if you visualized them in this sequence: melon-seesaw-lion. This sequence would translate to 352-0052. You should have remembered them as melon–lion–seesaw, because the correct number is 352–5200.

To prevent errors in translating Code Words to phone numbers, always see the first Code Word as the largest object in the link. The next Code Word should be associated with the first, but should be smaller. If you need a third Code Word, its object should be smaller than the second.

You will seldom need more than three Code Words for learning telephone numbers. The sizes of the objects in the link should be visualized without regard to their normal sizes.

For practice, cover the answers below. Convert the following sets of linked Code Words into their correct telephone numbers:

1. lion–seesaw–melon
2. seesaw–melon–lion
3. melon–seesaw–lion
4. melon–lion–seesaw
5. seesaw–lion–melon
6. lion–melon–seesaw

Answers:

1. 52/00/352
   520–0352

2. 00/3352/52
   003–5252

3. 352/00/52
   352–0052

4. 352/52/00
   352–5200

5. 00/52/352
   005-2352

6. 52/352/00
   523-5200

Note that changing the sequence of the three objects changed the numbers.

Complete the following exercise by changing the phone numbers into Code Words. I suggest that you try to develop a single Code Word for the prefixes and two Code Words for the suffixes, because most often this is how you will learn telephone numbers. Then look at the suggested Code Words that follow the exercise.

351-2214	532-3033	252-2543
(351-22-14)	(532-30-33)	(252-25-43)

432-7191	939-3225	357-8678
(432-71-91)	(939-32-25)	(357-86-78)

Some suggested Code Words are:

351 (mallet, malt, melt); 22 (nun); 14 (tire, tear, tour)
532 (lemon); 30 (moose, mice, maze); 33 (mom, mummy)
252 (nylon); 25 (nail); 43 (ram, rim, room)
432 (Roman); 71 (coat, cot, kit, kite); 91 (pit, boat, beet, bat)
939 (pump); 32 (moon, mane); 25 (nail)
357 (milk); 86 (fish); 78 (cuff, cave)

While remembering telephone numbers is a very practical application of the Number Code, it requires more practice, at first, than some of the other techniques. It is, however, a tremendous time-saver and an excellent practice exercise.

I suggest that you select the telephone numbers of twenty people or places you occasionally call but are not certain of their phone numbers. After confirming the numbers in the telephone directory, write the names and numbers on a plain sheet of paper. Then use the following approach:

1. Visualize the person or place.
2. Change the phone number into Code Words.
3. Associate the first Code Word with the person or place. Then link the remaining Code Words.

A VERY PRACTICAL EXERCISE FOR REMEMBERING TELEPHONE NUMBERS

Make a list of at least twenty names of people and places that may be important to you (doctor, teachers, coach, music instructor, pharmacy, or insurance agent).

Visualize each person or place, change the phone numbers to Code Words, and link the Code Words to the persons or places.

Cover the phone numbers. Look at the name of each person or place randomly and recall the phone number. Uncover the number to be sure you are correct. Later, during idle time, think of the names of the people or places and recall the phone numbers.

REMEMBERING DATES (YEARS)

Remembering dates is a frequent application of the Number Code. When it is important to know the year a certain event took place, there are a few simple rules that will help you eliminate 50 percent of the numbers to be remembered.

You can depend, to a great extent, on your natural memory and common sense. I'll give you a few examples of what I mean by common sense. These will be examples of information you are not likely to know or care about (with the possible exception of the sinking of the *Titanic*). Knowing how to remember this type of information is very important because it can be used in many applications. For example:

The parking meter was invented in 1935.
The air conditioner was invented in 1902.
The *Titanic* sank in 1912.
The safety elevator was invented in 1853.
The Crusades began in 1095.

Observe that there are only two things to remember: an event and a date. The common sense part of it is as follows: you would know that the parking meter would not have been invented before the car, and that the car had not been invented by 1835, so if the parking meter was invented in 35, it had to be **19**35.

- If the air conditioner was invented in 02, common sense would suggest that it was not 1802. It was **19**02.

- If you know anything about the sinking of the *Titanic,* common sense, again, would suggest that it was not in 1712 or 1812, so it had to be **19**12.

- Common sense might not tell some people whether the safety elevator was invented in 1853 (which seems much too early) or in 1953 (which seems much too late). You could

miss this one by 100 years, but common sense would not allow you to miss it by 1,000 years. Therefore, instead of using
just 53, you would use 853, just to avoid any confusion.

- You may not know in which century the Crusades began, but
  if you were interested enough in history to want to know
  that information, common sense would surely bring you
  within 1,000 years of the event.

The parking meter was invented in 1935.

1. See a parking meter.

2. For 1935, change 35 to a Code Word: **mule**.

3. Associate the **mule** with the parking meter. Visualize a parking
   meter with a **mule** standing on top of it! **Mule**=35 (19**35**).

The air conditioner was invented in 19**02**.

1. See the air conditioner.

2. Change 02 into a Code Word: **sun**.

3. Associate the **sun** with the air conditioner. Visualize the air
   conditioner with the **sun** coming out of it instead of air!
   sun=02 (19**02**).

The *Titanic* sank in 19**12**.

1. See the *Titanic*.

2. Change 12 into a Code Word: **tin**.

3. Associate the **tin** with the *Titanic*. Visualize the *Titanic*, made of **tin**. Maybe that's why it sank! **Tin**=12 (19**12**).

The safety elevator was invented in 1**853**.

1. See the safety elevator.

2. Change 853 into a Code Word: **film**.

3. Associate the **film** with the safety elevator. Visualize the safety elevator made of **film**! **Film**=853 (1**853**).

The Crusades began in 1**095**.

1. See the Crusades.

2. Change 095 into a Code Word: **spool**.

3. Associate the **spool** with the Crusades. Visualize each Crusader carrying a gigantic spool, so he could wind his way home after the Crusades! **Spool**=1095 (1095).

THE PRESIDENTS AND THEIR TERMS OF OFFICE

The Number Code can be used in combination with the other techniques to learn more complex information. For example, if you wanted to learn all of the presidents of the United States, the sequence in which they served, and their terms of office, you would use the numbered Cube, the audionym, association, the Number Code, and the Link system. It sounds complicated, but it is remarkably simple and easy. Following is a list of the presidents and their terms of office:

Sequence	President	Term of Office
1.	Washington	1789–97
2.	Adams	1797–1801
3.	Jefferson	1801–09
4.	Madison	1809–17
5.	Monroe	1817–25
6.	Adams	1825–29
7.	Jackson	1829–37
8.	Van Buren	1837–41
9.	Harrison	1841
10.	Tyler	1841–45
11.	Polk	1845–49
12.	Taylor	1849–50
13.	Fillmore	1850–53
14.	Pierce	1853–57
15.	Buchanan	1857–61
16.	Lincoln	1861–65
17.	Johnson	1865–69
18.	Grant	1869–77
19.	Hayes	1877–81
20.	Garfield	1881
21.	Arthur	1881–85
22.	Cleveland	1885–89
23.	Harrison	1889–93
24.	Cleveland	1893–97
25.	McKinley	1897–1901
26.	Roosevelt	1901–09
27.	Taft	1909–13
28.	Wilson	1913–21
29.	Harding	1921–23
30.	Coolidge	1923–29

Sequence	President	Term of Office
31.	Hoover	1929–33
32.	Roosevelt	1933–45
33.	Truman	1945–53
34.	Eisenhower	1953–61
35.	Kennedy	1961–63
36.	Johnson	1963–69
37.	Nixon	1969–74
38.	Ford	1974–77
39.	Carter	1977–81
40.	Reagan	1981–89
41.	Bush	1989–93
42.	Clinton	1993–2001
43.	Bush	2001–2008

I will show you how to learn the terms of all the presidents. You may want to learn just some of them. You should learn at least enough of them to understand how the system works for this type of information.

I recommend that you take time to learn *all* the presidents and their terms of office—even if you learn only a few at a time. It will give you a sense of accomplishment and it is an excellent practical example that uses all of the techniques you have learned so far. It would also be great as a family project to share with your children or grandchildren.

To learn any type of project information, you should always analyze it before you begin because it can eliminate a lot of unnecessary time and work. To learn the terms of office of each president, for example, there is no need to learn how long a president served. A new term begins on the same day the previous term ends, even in the event of the death of a president. You need learn only the year in which a president's term began, because you will know it ended when the next president took office.

It will also eliminate unnecessary work by knowing that only the first two presidents served in the 1700s. All the rest began their terms in the 1800s (until the twenty-sixth president, who entered office in 1901). Natural memory, common sense, and having some idea of when the president served will enable you to eliminate the first two digits from all of the four-digit dates.

Since you already know the names of the first nine presidents, by adding just one link to the audionym for each president, you will know the year he entered office. You will then know his complete term (because he served until the next president entered office).

At the time of writing of this book, there have been forty-three presidents. To learn all of the presidents and their terms using the Cube method, it will require five rooms (your Units Room as well as your 10s, 20s, 30s and 40s rooms).

1. See a **washing machine** in location 1—the back left corner of your Units room. The washing machine has a gigantic watch **f**ob bursting out of it! (I do not like to use **f**ob for this association because too many people don't know what a fob is. It is an ornament worn on a ribbon or chain for a pocket watch. The problem is that *fob* is the only useful word in the English language for number **89**.) Washington: 1**789**.

2. See the **ad** at location 2—the left wall of your Units room. The ad has a **book** (**97**) bursting out of it! **Adams: 1797.**

3. See a **chef** at location 3—the front left corner of your Units room. The **chef** is wearing a **suit** (**01**)! **Jefferson: 1801.**

4. See the **medicine** bursting out of location 4—the front wall of your Units room. The medicine is made of **soap** (**09**)! **Madison: 1809.**

5. See **money** bursting out of location 5—the front right corner of your Units room. The money has a **tack (17)** stuck in it! **Monroe: 1817.**

6. See an **ad** at location 6—the right wall of your Units room. The ad has a **nail (25)** stuck in it! **Adams: 1825.**

7. See a huge **jack** at location 7—the back right corner of your Units room. The jack has a gigantic **knob (29)** on it! **Jackson: 1829.**

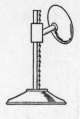

8. See a **van** bursting through location 8—the back wall of your Units room. The van has a **mik**e (**37**) stuck through it! **Van Buren: 1837.**

9. See **hair** growing out of the floor of your Units room! The hair has a **rat (41)** on it! **Harrison: 1841.**

10. See a gigantic **tile** sticking in the ceiling of your 10s room. The tile has a **rat (41)** on it! **Tyler: 1841.**

11. See **polka dots** at location 11—the back left corner of your 10s room. Each polka dot has a **reel (45)** on it! **Polk: 1845.**

12. See a **tail** sticking out of location 12—the left wall of your 10s room. The tail has a **rope (49)** around it! **Taylor: 1849.**

13. See a gigantic **film** at location 13—the front left corner of your 10s room. The film has a **lasso (50)** around it! **Fillmore: 1850.**

14. See a gigantic **purse** hanging at location 14—the front wall of your 10s room. The purse has a huge **lime (53)** in it! **Pierce: 1853.**

15. See a huge **blue cannon** bursting out of location 15—the front right corner of your 10s room. The blue cannon has a gigantic **lock (57)** sticking out of it! **Buchanan: 1857.**

16. See a gigantic **Lincoln penny** at location 16—the right wall of your 10s room. The Lincoln penny has a **sheet (61)** bursting out of it! **Lincoln: 1861.**

17. See a **john seat** (a toilet seat) hanging at location 17—the back right corner of your 10s room. The john seat is made of a **shell (65)** (a seashell). **Johnson: 1865.**

18. See a huge piece of **granite** bursting out of location 18—the back wall of your 10s room. The granite is carved into a **ship (69)**. **Grant: 1869.**

19. See a **haystack** at location 19—the floor of your 10s room. The haystack has a gigantic **cake (77)** in it! **Hayes: 1877.**

20. See a **garage door** at location 20—the ceiling of your 20s room. The garage door has a gigantic **foot (81)** stuck through it! **Garfield: 1881.**

21. See **artwork** bursting out of location 21—the back left corner of your 20s room. The artwork has a **foot (81)** stuck through it! **Arthur: 1881.**

22. See a gigantic **cleaver** stuck in location 22—the left wall of your 20s room. The cleaver has a huge **file (85)** stuck through it! **Cleveland: 1885.**

23. See **hair** growing out of location 23—the front left corner of your 20s room. The hair has a huge **f**ob **(89)** hanging from it! **Harrison: 18**89.

24. See a gigantic **cleaver** stuck in location 24—the front wall of your 20s room. This cleaver has a huge **pom**-pom **(93)** stuck through it! **Cleveland: 18**93.

25. See a gigantic **macaroni** bursting out of location 25—the front right corner of your 20s room. The macaroni has a **book (97)** stuck in it! **McKinley: 18**97.

26. See a huge rose growing out of location 26—the right wall of your 20s room. The rose is wearing a **suit (01)**! **Roosevelt: 1901.**

27. See gigantic pieces of **taffy** bursting out of location 27—the back right corner of your 20s room. The taffy is made of **soap (09)**! **Taft: 1909.**

28. See a gigantic **wheel** bursting out of location 28—the back wall of your 20s room. The wheel has a **tom**-tom **(13)** stuck in it! **Wilson: 1913.**

29. See a gigantic **heart** at location 29—the floor of your 20s room. The heart has a **net (21)** hanging on it! **Harding: 1921.**

30. See a **college** at location 30—the ceiling of your 30s room. The college has a gigantic jersey with your **name (23)** on it! **Coolidge: 1923.**

31. See a gigantic **hoof** hanging at location 31—the back left corner of your 30s room. The hoof has a huge k**nob (29)** on it! **Hoover: 1929.**

32. See a gigantic **rose** growing out of location 32—the left wall of your 30s room. The rose has a **mummy (33)** around it! **Roosevelt: 19**33.

33. See a **trooper** (a state trooper) at location 33—the front left corner of your 30s room. The trooper is holding a huge **reel (45)**! **Truman: 19**45.

34. See gigantic **eyes** at location 34—the front wall of your 30s room. Each eye has a huge **lime (53)** in it! **Eisenhower: 19**53.

35. See a gigantic **Kennedy half-dollar** at location 35—the front right corner of your 30s room. The Kennedy half-dollar has a **sheet (61)** bursting out of it! **Kennedy: 1961.**

36. See a huge **john seat** (a toilet seat) at location 36—the right wall of your 30s room. The john seat has a **chime (63)** hanging on it! **Johnson: 1963.**

37. See a gigantic **nickel** bursting out of location 37—the back right corner of your 30s room. The nickel has a **ship (69)** bursting through it! **Nixon: 1969.**

38. See a **Ford** bursting out of location 38—the back wall of your 30s room. The Ford has a gigantic **core (74)** bursting through the roof of it! **Ford: 1974.**

39. See a gigantic **cart** (a grocery cart) at location 39—the floor of your 30s room. The cart has a huge **cake (77)** in it! **Carter: 1977.**

40. See a gigantic **ray gun** (a gun that shoots rays) at location 40—the ceiling of your 40s room. The ray gun has a **foot (81)** coming out of it! **Reagan: 1981.**

41. See a gigantic **bush** growing at location 41—the back left corner of your 40s room. The bush has a huge f ob **(89)** hanging on it! **Bush: 1989.**

42. See a **clinic** at location 42—the left wall of your 40s room. The clinic has a gigantic **pom**-pom **(93)** sticking out of it! **Clinton: 1993.**

43. See a gigantic **bush** growing at location 43—the front left corner of your 40s room. The bush has a **suit (01)** hanging on it! **Bush: 2001.**

You have now seen how it is possible to learn information in sequence and also link other information to it. Again, you may not be interested in this particular information, but you should complete enough of the exercise to learn how to remember this type of information. There are many practical applications for this combination of techniques.

If you are learning the basic history of any nation, there are only three things you need to know to give you the entire chronological history of that nation. These things should be learned in sequence, beginning at the time that country came into being:

Who were the leaders?
When were they the leaders?
What happened when they were the leaders?

If you know these things, you will know more about the history of the nation than most well-educated natives of that country.

I recognize the value of knowing why certain historical events occurred. If desired, the *why* things happened could be added to the who, when, and what listed earlier. The important thing is that there is now an organized and effective way to quickly learn and remember the history of any nation.

In the case of the history of the United States, you can see how easy it is to learn the who and the when for all the presidents. The what happened could easily be added by using the Link system to include as many events as you wish. If you add the major historical events that occurred during each president's term of office, you would know the chronological history of the United States.

All of this information could be taught in a tiny fraction of the time it now takes to teach even a small part of it. I hope that because of the learning strategies you are discovering, tomorrow's students may be knowledgeable in the science of memory. If so, they could be taught with organized learning systems and will remember what they learn. Otherwise, learning by the inefficient method of repetition will continue.

THE KEY WORD SYSTEM (00–99)

You have already learned how to develop Code Words from numbers by using the Number Code. There are several advantages to having a Key Word that you always think of first for a number. A Key Word is a Code Word but, more than that, it is your favorite word (the one you consistently use for a particular number).

You should now develop Key Words for the numbers 00 through 99. In selecting your Key Words, you should choose the most common word for each of the 100 numbers.

I suggest that you use the following Key Words. If you wish to use any other word for a specific number, please be certain that you have a clear visual image of the object represented by the Key Word and that it does not cause any confusion with another Key Word. You will use the Key Words every day in practical applications of the system. I will give you two sets of Key Words. The first set is for the single-digit numbers 0 through 9.

NUMBER CODE

0 = S, C (soft), Z
1 = T, D, TH
2 = N
3 = M
4 = R
5 = L
6 = CH, SH, G (soft), J
7 = C (hard), K, G (hard), Q
8 = F, V, PH
9 = P, B

Following is a list of Key Words for all the single-digit numbers. Select just one word for each number and then always use that as your Key Word. Please note that the single-digit numbers are more difficult because each word must have only one consonant sound.

0   **s**ea, **s**ew (a needle), i**c**e, **z**oo, ho**s**e
1   **t**ea, **t**ie, **t**oe **t**ow (a tow truck), ha**t**
2   **N**oah (Noah's ark), k**n**ee, he**n**
3   **M**a, **m**ow (a lawn mower), ha**m**
4   **r**ye, hai**r**
5   **l**ei, **l**aw (a gavel), hai**l**
6   **Sh**oe, ha**sh**
7   **k**ey, hoo**k**
8   **f**oe (a competitor), hoo**f**, ha**lf** (a half-dollar). Please note that the *l* is silent.
9   **p**ie, **p**ea, hoo**p**

For the single-digit numbers I use:

hose,	hat,	hen,	ham,	hair,	hail,	hash,	hook,	hoof,	hoop
0	1	2	3	4	5	6	7	8	9

Following is a list of Key Words for all two-digit numbers:

KEY WORDS (00–99)

00 seesaw	20 nose	40 rose	60 cheese	80 face
01 suit	21 net	41 rat	61 sheet	81 fight
02 sun	22 nun	42 rain	62 chain	82 phone
03 sum	23 name	43 ram	63 chime	83 foam
04 sore	24 new oar	44 roar	64 chair	84 fur
05 sail	25 nail	45 reel	65 shell	85 file
06 sash	26 nacho	46 roach	66 choo-choo	86 fish
07 sock	27 neck	47 rock	67 check	87 fog
08 safe	28 knife	48 roof	68 chef	88 fife
09 soap	29 knob	49 rope	69 ship	89 fob
10 toes	30 moose	50 lasso	70 case	90 bus
11 tote	31 mat	51 light	71 coat	91 bat
12 tuna	32 moon	52 lion	72 cone	92 bone
13 team	33 mummy	53 lime	73 comb	93 bum
14 tire	34 mower	54 lure	74 car	94 bear
15 tail	35 mail	55 lily	75 coal	95 bell
16 teach	36 match	56 leash	76 cash	96 beach
17 tack	37 mike	57 lock	77 Coke	97 book
18 taffy	38 muff	58 loaf	78 cuff	98 beef
19 top	39 mop	59 lip	79 cap	99 pipe

Following is a description of what I see for the 100 Key Words. I'll skip obvious ones.

00 see saw
01 suit
02 sun
03 sum (a calculator)
04 sore (a bandage)

05 sail
06 sash (an ornamental scarf worn around the waist)
07 sock
08 safe
09 soap

10 toes
11 tot (a child)
12 tuna (a live tuna fish)
13 team (your favorite team)
14 tire

15 tail
16 teach (a teacher you know or knew)
17 tack
18 taffy
19 top (a child's spinning toy)

20 nose
21 net
22 nun
23 name (a nameplate)
24 new oar (an oar with a price tag on it)

25 nail
26 nacho
27 neck
28 knife
29 nap (bed)

30 moose
31 mat
32 moon
33 mummy
34 mower

35 mail
36 match (the t is silent)
37 mike
38 muff (an earmuff)
39 mop

40 rose
41 rat
42 rain
43 ram
44 roar (a rocket)

45 reel
46 roach
47 rock
48 roof
49 rope

50 lasso
51 light (a lightbulb)

52   lion
53   lime
54   lure (a fishing lure)

55   lily
56   leash
57   lock
58   loaf
59   lip

60   cheese
61   sheet
62   chain
63   chime
64   chair

65   shell
66   choo-choo
67   check
68   chef
69   ship

70   case
71   coat
72   cone
73   comb
74   car

75   coal
76   cash
77   Coke

78   cuff
79   cap

80   fuse
81   foot (not to be confused with toes for number 10)
82   fan
83   foam
84   fur

85   file (a nail file)
86   fish
87   fog
88   fife
89   fob (a watch fob)

90   bus
91   bat
92   bone
93   bum
94   bear

95   bell
96   beach
97   book
98   beef
99   pipe

Notice that the Key Words for all of the teens begin with *t*. All of the twenties begin with *n*, the 30s begin with *m*, and so on. In addition, since each block of ten numbers ends with 0 through 9, you can almost guess what the Key Words will be. For example, all of the seventies begin with *c* and end with the assigned sound for each of the numbers 0 through 9:

70	C-S	case
71	C-T	coat
72	C-N	cone
73	C-M	comb
74	C-R	car
75	C-L	coal
76	C-SH	cash
77	C-K	cake
78	C-FF	cuff
79	C-P	cap

As you review your list of Key Words, you may not know which of the consonant sounds is to be used for a particular number, but you do know that any number can be converted to like-consonant sounds, and that should get you close enough to the Key Word to know what it is. Soon, you will make the translation without much thought, but that comes with a little practice.

Your success in remembering numbers will depend on your mastering the Number Code and, to a large extent, on your knowing the Key Words.

A GREAT PRACTICAL APPLICATION
FOR THE KEY WORD SYSTEM

Find out the birthdate of each of your family members and some of your friends. Use the following format for the date: mm/dd/yy. Each date can quickly be changed to three key words. Let's suggest that Daniel's birthdate is July 15, 1979. Change the date to this format: 07/15/79. Using the Key Words, 07/15/79 converts to **sock-tail-cap**. Just imagine Daniel holding a gigantic sock! The sock has a huge tail sticking out of it! The tail has a cap on the end of it! Later, when you think of Daniel and recall the **sock**, **tail**, and **cap** (in that order), you will know Daniel's birthday and how old he is.

This is a great practical application of several of the techniques you have learned so far. You should practice this exercise by applying it to at least twenty family members and friends.

DEMONSTRATE YOUR MEMORY POWER: A LONG-DIGIT NUMBER

After you know the Key Words for every two-digit number, you can demonstrate to yourself and others one of the most amazing examples of the power of a trained memory. In fact, this demonstration is so impressive that I sometimes hesitate to include it in my lectures. I don't want my audiences to confuse education with entertainment. The truth is, the demonstration is incredibly entertaining. In fact, based on the reaction I always receive from an audience, it's downright mind-boggling! What others do not know is that anybody can learn how to do it quickly and easily. The demonstration involves remembering a long-digit number after seeing or hearing it only one time.

According to psychologists, the average individual can recall only a seven-digit number after hearing it once. With my learning system, you can recall a twenty-digit, forty-digit, 100-digit number, or more, after seeing or hearing it only once. Even better, you can do it with ease and self-confidence. I know this sounds incredible. It's not only incredible—it's really easy with an organized memory system!

I can think of only two reasons to recall a long-digit number: First, to show off! There is nothing wrong with showing off the incredible power of your mind just as you would show off a magic trick. Second, it is one of the best mental exercises you can perform because you can precisely measure your accuracy and speed.

I urge you to learn this exercise for several very important reasons: it will require you to know the Key Words for the numbers 00 through 99. Also, it will greatly benefit you when you need to remember numbers for any other memory project involving numbers. Further, it will enable you to practice the use of the following memory tools anytime, anywhere!

The numbered Cube system
The Number Code
The Key Words
The association

I often practice the long-digit number during "waiting" times. This is a way of making good use of time I might otherwise waste. If you were to keep track, you would be amazed to discover how many of your valuable moments are spent waiting for things to happen: for public transportation, for people to see you at appointments, and so on. By practicing memory exercises, you can effectively turn waiting rooms into classrooms.

With a trained memory, you will even begin to look forward to those times you may once have dreaded. I like to go through such mental gymnastics while traveling. In addition to the practical value of the mental exercise, I find it very relaxing while driving or on an airplane.

There is probably no better confidence-builder among memory students than to demonstrate their ability to recall a long-digit number. If I were your memory doctor I would prescribe at least a forty-digit number every day for the rest of your life. It will build your self-confidence. The practice will increase your memory efficiency and, therefore, your memory power, and help you to stay mentally alert for a lifetime! In addition, the long-digit number exercise will sharpen your concentration skills. You cannot accurately recall different forty-digit numbers every day without, at the same time, improving your ability to concentrate. The exercise will also enhance your self-image and consistently improve your memory abilities. Both will enable you to gain the respect of others.

Before you can rapidly store a long-digit number just by hearing it, it is necessary to know the Key Words for the numbers 00 through 99. This is because you store the numbers two digits at a time. Assuming that you do not yet know all of the Key Words, I will tell you in advance which two-digit numbers I am going to use for this sample exercise.

Since this is your first experience with the long-digit number, I will give you only twenty digits to remember. That sounds like an ambitious first step, but soon you will see how simple it really is.

To perform this memory feat, all you need is the Cube and the Key Words. You won't even need the numbered locations—just the sequence of the numbered locations.

Let's suggest that you already know the Key Words for the following two-digit numbers:

53 **lime**	21 **net**
14 **tire**	32 **moon**
22 **nun**	10 **toes**
40 **rose**	52 **lion**
25 **nail**	20 **nose**

Practice these two-digit numbers until you are certain that you know the Key Words and can see an object for each of them.

52	40	21	22	20
32	10	25	14	53

Please do not continue until you know the Key Words for these two-digit numbers.

When you are demonstrating a multidigit number, always have the person or persons give you the number in sets of two. You should always ask them to allow you to control the speed by waiting for you to repeat the number before they give you another set.

For this demonstration, use your Units room or the room in which you are now located. Also, always start with the ceiling location so that you can store ten sets of numbers (twenty digits) in each room.

Visualize the ceiling of the room. Look up at it right now. You should be looking at or visualizing the ceiling.

The first number is **21**. For 21, think 2-1, N–T, **net**. See a gigantic **net** hanging from the ceiling.

As soon as you see a clear mental image of the net at the ceiling, mentally see the next location (the back left corner), and wait for the next number.

The next number is **32**. Think 3-2, M–N, **moon**. See the moon rolling through the back left corner! It is crushing everything in its way! See it! Hear it! Look out! Moon!

After I mentally store a two-digit number I always review the previous location to confirm what I put there. Then I review the present location by seeing what I put there. Then, I look at the next location and wait for the next number.

Do that now. Look up at the ceiling and see the **net**. This will be the last time you will look at the ceiling and see the **net** while you are learning the number.

Next, review the back left corner again and see the **moon**.

Now look at the left wall and wait for the next two-digit number.

The next number is **25**. Think 2-5, N-L, **n**a**il**. See the largest nail in the world being driven toward you through the left wall! Hear it!

Review the back-left corner and see the **moon**. Review the present location and see the **nail**. See the next location—the front left corner—and wait for the next number.

The next number is **22**. Think 2-2, N-N, **nun**. See a nun standing in the front left corner of the room! The nun is so tall that she reaches from the floor to the ceiling!

Review the left wall and see the **nail**. Review the present location and see the **nun**. See the next location—the front wall.

The next number is **52**. Think 5-2, L-N, **lion**. See a gigantic lion leaping through the front wall! It is leaping right at you!

Review the front left corner and see the **nun**. Review the present location and see the **lion**. See the next location (the front right corner).

The next number is **14**. Think 1-4, T-R, **tire**. See an unbelievably large tire crashing through the front right corner of the room! Hear it as it spins and crashes through the front right corner!

Review the front wall and see the **lion**. Review the present location and see the **tire**. See the next location—the right wall.

The next number is **20**. Think 2-0, N-S, **nose**. See a huge nose at the right wall!

Review the front right corner and see the **tire**. Review the present location and see the **nose**. See the next location—the back right corner.

The next number is **43**. Think 4-3, R-M, **ram**. See the largest ram in the world bursting through the back right corner! It is kicking everything in its way!

Review the right wall and see the **nose**. Review the present location and see the **ram**. See the next location (the back wall).

The next number is **53**. Think 5-3, L-M, **lime**. See a gigantic lime so large that it fills the entire back wall of the room!! It is squirting lime juice all over you!

Review the back right corner and see the **ram**. Review the present location and see the **lime**. See the next location—the floor.

The next number is **40**. Think 4-0, R-S, **rose**. See a giant rose growing out of the floor! You can even smell it!

Review the back wall and see the **lime**. Review the present location and see the **rose**.

Now, if you saw a clear visual image of each object as we went around the room, you should be able to start at the ceiling and move around the room, identifying each object along the way.

To remember the twenty-digit number, just translate the ten objects (Key Words) back to their two-digit numbers! Here is the process:

Ceiling: See the **net**.
Think: N-T.
Say: 2-1.

Please note that, you will say each digit separately. Don't say "21"; instead say "2, 1." It is much more impressive to call the numbers back as twenty single digits rather than ten sets of two-digit numbers.

Back left corner: See **moon**. Think M-N. Say 3-2.
Left wall: See **nail**. Think N-L. Say 2-5.
Front left corner: See **nun**. Think N-N. Say 2-2.
Front wall: See **lion**. Think L-N. Say 5-2.

Front right corner: See **tir**e. Think T-R. Say 1-4.

Right wall: See **n**ose. Think N-S. Say 2-0.

Back right corner: See **ram**. Think R-M. Say 4-3.

Back wall: See **lim**e. Think L-M. Say 5-3.

Floor: See **ro**se. Think R-S. Say 4-0.

Now, try it on your own! Without looking at the book, start at the ceiling and write down the ten sets (twenty digits) in sequence. Then come back to this page and check your answers:

21	32	25	22	52	14	20	43	53	40

How did you do? Considering that this was the first time you ever even tried to do it, I'll bet you did pretty well. After you are certain you know the Key Words for all 100 numbers (00-99), practice taking at least a twenty-digit number every day. Soon you will use two rooms to store forty-digit numbers. After you have filled the first room (ending with the floor), just think of your next room and start at the ceiling. Repeat the process of visualizing an object in each of the ten locations within the room. I usually demonstrate a forty-digit number.

A 100-digit number would fill five rooms. Because you will be using your rooms to store the objects, soon you will be able to mentally move around each room very rapidly. When doing the long number exercise, you don't need to think of the locations as being numbered. Just start at the ceiling, then the back left corner, then the left wall, and so on. Soon, you will automatically visualize the ceiling, back left corner, and left wall, in sequence without much thought.

As you visualize objects in each of the locations within your rooms, include in your image everything in that area of the room.

For example, if there is a TV in the corner of the room, then you should associate the Key Word (or whatever data you are storing) to the TV, not just to the corner itself.

I use the kitchen of a previous residence for my 30s room. My location 37 is not really the back right corner—it is the refrigerator that was located in the back right corner. When I associate any data with location 37, I do not associate it with the back right corner in my kitchen, I associate it with my refrigerator that was located there.

Every time you use the Cube system, it will be easier. You will never have been more aware of your rooms and the things you have in them than when you begin using the Cube system.

Every time you store a long-digit number, it will be easier because you will become more familiar with the 100 objects represented by the Key Words. Everyone thinks they are giving you a long-digit number to remember. Actually, they are giving you your own objects that you can place in your own rooms.

The nice part about taking a long-digit number is that there can be no surprises—not if you know all of the Key Words (00–99). There will be those who will try to trick you by giving you the same number twice. Relax! If you can see a net on the ceiling, you can see a net at any other location!

Nearly every time I demonstrate a long-digit number, which is usually forty digits, the audience will give me combinations like 01 followed by 10. They think that I will be confused, but you and I know that 01 (**suit**) looks nothing like 10 (**toes**)! After I have demonstrated a long number, I wait a few minutes and then recall the number backward.

When taking a long-digit number from others, you must always be in charge! Don't let anyone rush you. Never take the next set of two digits without clearly visualizing the one you have just heard.

Occasionally, you will be asked to immediately take another

long number. If this happens, don't use the same room or rooms for the next demonstration. Why take the chance of seeing two objects in the same location? You can use the same room(s) as often as you wish, as long as it is not done immediately. I would not try to store two long-digit numbers in the same room within several hours of each other.

I consider a long-digit number a mental exercise. It is not something I want to keep any longer than it takes to call it back to the person who gave it to me. It is temporary information, and I treat it that way by ignoring it after I have recalled it. The information will remain for several hours or days whether I want it to or not. Unless you plan to recite the number again, don't try to remember it.

Long-term and short-term information are treated alike, but with one exception: short-term information is simply ignored immediately after it is used. Long-term information should be reviewed immediately after it is learned, then periodically with greater time between each review (the next day, one week, one month, six months, and so on).

Most students use my suggested 100 Key Words, but prefer to create their own visual images for each of them. Your own images will be much more real than any illustration I can give you in a book. If, for example, you use **car** for 74, surely you will visualize a different car than the one I see. Also, it is better to use a real car than a drawing of a car.

Step 7

THE TOPOGRAPH SYSTEM

The Topograph system has many uses. I first developed this concept when I was creating my course on the human skeleton in 1976. With the Topograph system, students learn the names and locations of all 206 bones of the human skeleton in only ninety minutes! The Topograph system is used when you want to learn the names and locations of the parts within a whole. For example:

- Classroom seating charts
- Names of players by position on a team
- Street layouts of towns and cities
- Layout of a grocery store
- Location of notes on a musical instrument
- The bones within the body
- The anatomical names and locations
- The countries within a continent or region of the world
- The states within a nation
- The parts within an engine
- The parts within an engine part
- The rivers within a country

- The parts of any machine or equipment
- The instrument panel of a plane

GEOGRAPHY

The Topograph system is designed to be used when you want to know the physical parts of anything in relation to the whole unit. This is the system I use to teach geography. With this system, you can learn and remember the name and location of every country in the world in less than six hours.

This system is fast, fun, and easy! Above all, it is incredibly practical because it can be used in thousands of applications. As an example for this book, I have chosen geography and the region of Central America. Here is an outline map of the seven countries of Central America:

The first step is to change the name of each country to an audionym. Following are the audionyms I use for the countries of Central America.

COUNTRIES OF CENTRAL AMERICA

Country	Audionym
Belize	bells
Guatemala	guacamole
El Salvador	elephant
Honduras	honeydew
Nicaragua	nickel
Costa Rica	coaster
Panama	pan

Please be certain you know these seven audionyms before continuing.

The next step is to see each audionym in the area of the country it represents. The physical relationship of the audionyms to one another provides an incredibly effective visual system for remembering the names, locations, and physical relationships of the countries they represent. Look at the audionyms in place on this outline map of Central America.

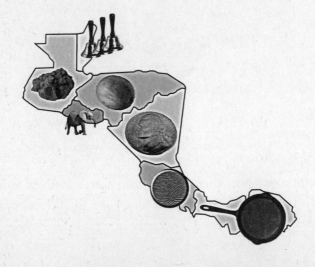

HOW TO REMEMBER THE NAMES AND
LOCATIONS OF THE COUNTRIES *WITHOUT* A MAP

To remember the names of the countries of Central America without using a map, first see the following map with a line drawn from the northernmost country to the southeasternmost country, just like you would read the pages of a book. In this case, the northernmost country is Belize. Notice that the line generally follows a north-to-south and west-to-east course. I call this a sequence map. The map puts the countries into the following sequence: Belize; Guatemala; El Salvador; Honduras; Nicaragua; Costa Rica; and Panama.

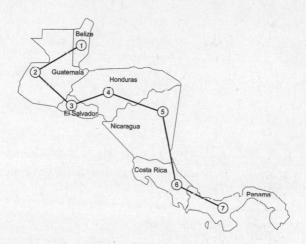

To establish the known—what you will know about the region of Central America when you want to recall all the countries—start with the northernmost country, Belize. Use the Link system to connect the audionyms for all of the countries.

Imagine the **bells** with **guacamole** pouring out of them!
Imagine the **guacamole** with an **elephant** standing in it!

Imagine the **elephant** holding a gigantic **honeydew**!

Imagine the **honeydew** with a huge **nickel** stuck in it!

Imagine the **nickel** turning into a **coaster**!

Imagine the **coaster** with a **pan** on it!

With your point finger, trace the ovals on each of the countries, starting with Belize. As you trace each oval, think, "Bells, Belize; guacamole, Guatemala; elephant, El Salvador. . . ."

Now, trace each oval, without the map, in the order of the sequence map, saying each audionym and the country it represents.

You should now be able to use a plain sheet of paper, without any reference, and draw the seven ovals representing the seven countries of Central America. The ovals should represent the name, location, and relative size of each country. When you can do this, you truly know the name of every country in the region, where it is located, and its relative size.

THE GRID SYSTEM

The Grid system has a lot of versatility because it is adjustable to the size of a project. The grid is always set up as a square or a rectangle with alpha characters down the left side to identify the rows and numeric characters across the top to identify the columns.

Code Words are created in each block of the grid using the alpha symbols down the left side and the numeric symbols across the top of the grid.

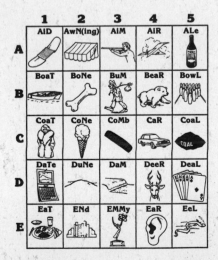

	1	2	3	4	5
A	AiD	AwN(ing)	AiM	AiR	ALe
B	BoaT	BoNe	BuM	BeaR	BowL
C	CoaT	CoNe	CoMb	CaR	CoaL
D	DaTe	DuNe	DaM	DeeR	DeaL
E	EaT	ENd	EMMy	EaR	EeL

Each Code Word, when used in the grid, becomes a topical location. For location C-2, the Code Word would begin with C and include the consonant N (for 2). **Can**, **cone**, or **cane** would work.

For A=1 (**Aid**), see the Band-**Aid** on a specific arm of a specific person. For location E-4, see a specific **ear** on a specific person.

A grid can be set up for any number of squares. When I use it, I normally set it up for only twenty-five locations, as in the illustration on page 114.

A very practical application of the grid system is its flexible use for presentations. If your presentation is made up of fifteen major topics, you could set up a sixteen-square (4 × 4) grid. If you want to cover thirty major points in a presentation, you could set up a rectangular grid (5 squares times 6 squares).

In recalling the information in a grid, just move across the top row from left to right: A-1, A-2, A-3, and so on. You will know when you get to the end of the row. Then, recall rows B, C, D, and so on. I suggest that you begin by storing information in a nine- or sixteen-square grid (3 × 3 or 4 × 4).

You may wish to practice the use of the grid system by storing nine or sixteen random objects. You could even store two-digit numbers in each square by using your Key Words.

After you have stored the information randomly, you will be able to recall it in linear sequence. In fact, you will be able to recall it forward, backward, or diagonally! This adjustable system can be used instead of the Cube system, although it does not have the Cube's advantage of sequentially numbering the information.

The grid system will give you another tool from which to choose when working on any memory project. It is organized, it is simple, and it is effective. It is an excellent tool for giving a presentation, because it can be tailor-made for the number of topics in your talk.

USE YOUR MEMORY TO DEVELOP CONCENTRATION

You say you have trouble concentrating? Surely, you know the value of being able to concentrate, but how do you learn to do it? How can you practice it? And how can you prove to yourself or anybody else that you are actually concentrating?

This chapter has a special exercise for practicing concentration. Complete the exercise and practice it frequently. You will be amazed at the dramatic improvement in your ability to concentrate. Even better, as you continue to practice, your ability to concentrate will improve dramatically. The exercise has a built-in measuring device so you can accurately monitor your progress.

One hot summer morning a long time ago, I got a call from one of the most successful head coaches in the history of professional football. He had seen me on a TV talk show and wondered if I could apply my memory techniques to concentration. I immediately said, "Yes, sir!" Only after I hung up did I begin to figure out how I could go about actually doing it. I had never found a project to which my learning systems could not be successfully applied, so I felt confident in giving an immediate and positive response. I was, however, surprised at the request for a memory technique to teach professional football players to concentrate. I would have expected him to ask me to teach the players to remember their plays.

I soon discovered that these big guys are also bright guys. Remembering plays was not a problem for them. The coach wanted to maximize his successes by minimizing his team's errors. To do that, they had to learn to keep their minds on business.

Only the fans call professional football a game. Those who are responsible for making a profit from pro ball, and whose financial futures depend on its success, call football a business. There are few businesses in which organization and concentration are more critical.

In any business, of course, it is important to keep our minds on what we are doing. But in the business of football, it is especially important because everything happens so much faster. Even the slightest break in concentration can be extremely costly. If a player's mind wanders from business at the wrong instant, even for a split second, it can mean a sudden and drastic change in that individual's professional status and in the team's overall success. A lack of concentration can come right down to a question of Super Bowl or superbomb. It can determine the color of the ink used in the profit-and-loss column.

Within two days of the coach's call, I reported to the summer training camp with my concentration exercise. I was positive the system would work and I was excited about the technique. Not only would it help my favorite NFL team and my favorite coach, but it would also help millions of others to develop an extremely useful skill.

Developing the power to concentrate is exactly the same as developing any other skill. It takes practice. We exercise our bodies to have well-toned muscles. We practice a musical instrument to become skilled at it. Concentration is no different. If we want to teach ourselves to focus on a single thought or goal, we have to practice by doing it.

THE TOUR OF THE KNIGHT

The mental exercise I designed for improving concentration uses a chessboard and the chess piece known as the Knight. I call this exercise the Tour of the Knight. It is accomplished with a paper and pencil.

In chess, each piece has specific moves that it must make. The Knight must jump two squares in one direction and one square in another, forming an L.

Below you see the Knight and all of its possible moves. Notice that the Knight can move only in the following directions:

Left two, up one.
Left two, down one.
Up two, left one.
Up two, right one.
Right two, up one.
Right two, down one.
Down two, right one.
Down two, left one.

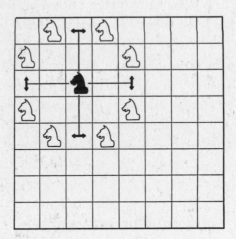

Centuries ago, someone developed a way to move the Knight into all sixty-four squares of the chessboard without touching any of the same squares twice. The following illustration shows the Tour of the Knight, starting and ending on any square.

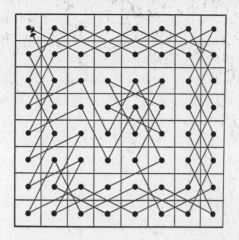

Even if you know nothing about the game of chess, this is an excellent exercise to improve your concentration skills.

The Tour of the Knight may not seem to have much going for it in practical application. But remember, we are not talking about the games of chess or football. We are talking about concentration. The exercising of our concentration "muscles" could just as easily be applied to any field where it is important to keep our minds on what we are doing.

Events that determine our value within an organization can change in no more time than it takes to miss an important point in a sales presentation because we were not concentrating. In the case of pro ball, a missed pass is the equivalent of a sale not made or a deal not concluded profitably.

To make a long story slightly longer, the team did learn the Tour of the Knight in only a few hours. Many reported it helped them with their concentration and the team finished in the NFL playoffs that season. Since then, many thousands of students have dramatically improved their ability to concentrate by learning and using this exercise.

Concentration is critical to success. The ability to concentrate can be instrumental in developing the ability to fix your attention on a goal. Ultimately, that may mean the difference between being a salesperson and being a *top* salesperson. It can be the difference between making a living—and making a fortune! It can help a person become a treasured employee. In academic life, concentration can make the difference between tolerable grades and being an honor student. The ability to concentrate, in short, can push you off the fence—and into greener pastures.

The remainder of this chapter is dedicated to one objective: to teach you *how to concentrate!* Please follow the exercise very carefully. Once you have learned the system, you will not only have learned a practical exercise for improving your concentration, you will have learned how to give a mind-boggling demonstration of memory power!

After studying this project for a while, I thought of a way to perform the demonstration without looking at the chessboard while doing it. It is more impressive to do it without looking at the board and it requires tremendous concentration. This mental exercise will develop your ability to concentrate and will also enable you to measure your results. If you make even one mistake, you will be unable to complete the tour.

Do you remember the game you may have played as a child in which each person in a circle had to remember, in sequence, the item mentioned by each previous person in the circle? The process continued as the number of items increased. Individuals who missed an item were eliminated from the circle.

This exercise works in the same way except that you will use a memory technique to recall sixty-four items. The last item will be linked to the first item to complete the "circle." You will be able to start with any item in the circle and recall, in sequence, the sixty-four items.

BLACK

	a	b	c	d	e	f	g	h	
8	a8	b8	c8	d8	e8	f8	g8	h8	8
7	a7	b7	c7	d7	e7	f7	g7	h7	7
6	a6	b6	c6	d6	e6	f6	g6	h6	6
5	a5	b5	c5	d5	e5	f5	g5	h5	5
4	a4	b4	c4	d4	e4	f4	g4	h4	4
3	a3	b3	c3	d3	e3	f3	g3	h3	3
2	a2	b2	c2	d2	e2	f2	g2	h2	2
1	a1	b1	c1	d1	e1	f1	g1	h1	1
	a	b	c	d	e	f	g	h	

WHITE

Each block on the chessboard has an "address," starting with the letter of the column and ending with the number of the rank, such as a1, h8, and so on. Likewise, each block has a picture whose name starts with the letter of the column and whose next consonant sound is a conversion of the Number Code to a letter. Coordinate c5 can be converted to **coal**. Conversely, **coal** can be converted to c5.

Sixty-four links will be formed with the last link connected to the first link, thereby completing a circuit. This enables you to start on any square (link) and end up back at the same square (link).

Following is the link of sixty-four pictures. I suggest that you learn at least ten links at a time. When you are certain you know the links, continue with at least ten more, repeating the process until you can recall the sixty-four links without missing any of them.

See a bottle of **af**tershave (**a8**) with a **ca**ke (**c7**) on it!

See the **ca**ke with an **ev**ergreen (**e8**) on it!

See the **e**vergreen (**e8**) with **g**oggles (**g7**) on it!

See the **g**oggles (**g7**) with **h**ail (**h5**) on it!

See the **h**ail (**h5**) with **g**um (**g3**) on it!

See the **g**um (**g3**) with a **h**at (**h1**) on it!

See the **h**at (**h1**) with a **f**an (**f2**) on it!

See the **f**an (**f2**) with a gigantic **d**ate (**d1**) on it!

See the **d**ate (**d1**) with a **b**one (**b2**) stuck in it!

See the **b**one (**b2**) with a **c**ar (**c4**) bursting out of it!

See the **c**ar (**c4**) with an **am**bulance (**a3**) on top of it!

See the **am**bulance (**a3**) with a gigantic **b**ell (**b5**) on it!

See the **b**ell (**b5**) with a gigantic **ac**robat (**a7**) as a gong!

See the **ac**robat (**a7**) with a **c**uff (**c8**) on it!

See the **c**uff (**c8**) with an **e**gg (**e7**) on it!

See the **e**gg (**e7**) with a **g**avel (**g8**) stuck in it!

See the **g**avel (**g8**) a **h**itch (a trailer hitch) (**h6**) on it!

See the **h**itch (**h6**) with a **g**ear (**g4**) on it!

See the **g**ear (**g4**) with a **h**en (**h2**) on it!

See the **h**en (**h2**) with a gigantic **f**oot (**f1**)!

See the **f**oot (**f1**) with an **E**mmy (**e3**) on it!

See the **E**mmy (**e3**) with a **f**ile (**f5**) stuck through it!

See the **f**ile (**f5**) with a **d**ish (**d6**) on it!

See the **d**ish (**d6**) with an **e**ar (**e4**) on it!

See the **e**ar (**e4**) with a **f**ish (**f6**) on it!

See the **f**ish (**f6**) with a **d**oll (**d5**) in its mouth!

See the **d**oll (**d5**) wearing a **f**ur (**f4**)!

See the **f**ur (**f4**) with **e**tched (**e6**) glass all over it!

See the **e**tched (**e6**) glass with a **d**eer (**d4**) standing on it!

See the **d**eer (**d4**) with **c**ash (**c6**) piled on it!

See the **c**ash (**c6**) with an **al**bum (**a5**) on it!

See the **al**bum (**a5**) with a **b**ike (**b7**) on it!

See the **b**ike (**b7**) with a **d**ove (**d8**) on it!

See the dove (d8) with a factory (f7) on it!

See the factory (f7) with a gigantic hoof (h8) on it!

See the hoof (h8) with a gauge (g6) on it!

See the gauge (g6) with hair (h4) growing out of it!

See the hair (h4) with a gun (g2) in it!

See the gun (g2) with an eatery (e1) (a restaurant) on it!

See the eatery (e1) with a huge can (c2) in it!

See the can (c2) with an attic (a1) in it!

See the attic (a1) with a bum (b3) in it!

See the bum (b3) wearing a gigantic coat (c1)!

See the coat (c1) with envelopes (e2) all over it!

See the envelopes (e2) with a gate (g1) on them!

See the gate (g1) with a ham (h3) on it!

See the ham (h3) with a gull (g5) (a seagull) on it!

See the gull (g5) with a hog (h7) on it!

See the hog (h7) playing a fife (f8)!

See the fife (f8) with a duck (d7) on it!

See the duck (d7) with beef (b8) on it!

See the beef (b8) with ash (a6) on it!

See the ash (a6) with a bear (b4) in it!

See the bear (b4) with an awning (a2) on it!

See the awning (a2) with a comb (c3) on it!

See the comb (c3) with a boat (b1) on it!

See the boat (b1) with a den (d2) in it!

See the den (d2) with foam (f3) in it!

See the foam (f3) with an eel (e5) in it!

See the eel (e5) with a dam (d3) on it!

See the dam (d3) with coal (c5) on it!

See the coal (c5) with an airplane (a4) on it!

See the airplane (a4) with a beach (b6) on it!

See the beach (b6) with aftershave (a8) on it!

Cover the list and look at the first coordinate and word. It translates to the coordinate at the left. Recall the next word and its coordinate, and so on. Uncover to check your answers:

a8   **af**tershave

c7   **ca**ke

e8   **ev**ergreen

g7   **gogg**les

h5   **hail**

g3   **gum**

h1   **hat**

f2   **fan**

d1   **date**

b2   **bone**

c4   **car**

a3   **am**bulance

b5   **bell**

a7   **ac**robat

c8   **cuff**

e7   **egg**

g8   **ga**vel

h6   **hitch** (a trailer hitch)

g4   **gear**

h2   **hen**

f1   **foot**

e3   **Emm**y

f5   **file**

d6   **dish**

e4   **ear**

f6   **fish**

d5   **doll**

f4   **fur**

e6 **etch**

d4 **deer**

c6 **cash**

a5 **al**bum

b7 **bike**

d8 **dove**

f7 **f**actory

h8 **hoof**

g6 **gauge**

h4 **hair**

g2 **gun**

e1 **eatery** (a restaurant)

c2 **can**

a1 **at**tic

b3 **bum**

c1 **coat**

e2 **en**velopes

g1 **gate**

h3 **ham**

g5 **gull** (a seagull)

h7 **hog**

f8 **fif**e

d7 **duck**

b8 **beef**

a6 **ash**

b4 **bear**

a2 **awning**

c3 **comb**

b1 **boat**

d2 **den**

f3 **f**oam

e5 **eel**

d3   **d**a**m**

c5   **c**oa**l**

a4   **air**plane

b6   **b**ea**ch**

a8   **af**tershave

The link you have just completed will give you the "address" (coordinate) of each move to place the Knight into all sixty-four squares of the chessboard. To practice, draw a square on a piece of paper, chalkboard, or flip chart. Divide the square in half, both horizontally and vertically. That will give you four squares. Divide the four squares in half both horizontally and vertically. That will give you sixteen squares. Divide the remaining squares in half both horizontally and vertically. That will give you sixty-four squares, the number of squares on a chessboard.

You may think it is unnecessary to illustrate a method for dividing a large square into sixty-four squares, but if you ever demonstrate the Tour of the Knight in public it is best to know that the squares are all going to be at least approximately the same size.

At first, you may want to complete the exercise yourself (that is, while looking at the squares). Soon, however, you should allow someone else to mark the squares while you move the Knight without looking at the board.

When someone else marks the squares for you, tell them to put a dot in the center of the upper left square (a8) and to place their point finger on the dot. Then, tell them to put a dot at the center of the square at c7 and draw a straight line to connect the two dots. They should then place their point finger on the dot at c7 and wait for you to tell them where to put the next dot.

Continue the process until you complete the exercise. You will end on the same square on which you began. Because the tour makes a complete circuit, you can start and finish on any square.

Whether or not you play chess, this is an excellent mental exercise both for memory and to develop your power of concentration. Too often, there are those who allow their minds to coast. They don't exercise their minds because no one has ever taught them how to do it.

I challenge you to exercise your mind every day just as you should exercise your body. Mental exercise is just as important as physical exercise. In fact, long after you have lost the stamina for strenuous physical activity, you can still have the mental strength and alertness to outdistance those who failed to develop the power of their minds. I encourage you to exercise your mind and your body in order to develop and maintain both physical and mental fitness.

You may wish to draw about six chessboards on a standard 8½-by-11 sheet of paper and then have some copies made in order to practice this most beneficial exercise.

Step 9

HOW TO REMEMBER NAMES

In seminars I have conducted for more than three decades, I always ask students what particular area of their own memories they would most like to improve. At least 90 percent of them answer, "Remembering names!"

As I began compiling my years of experience in training students to remember, I got to the names section and came to a startling realization. On one hand, to give you all of the information needed to properly and adequately learn to remember names would require an entire volume on that subject alone. On the other hand, to give you nothing at all on names amounts to a serious omission from a book on memory-training.

I have chosen to treat the subject as fully as possible here, but with the understanding that there is a great deal more to learning how to become an expert at remembering names than I could do justice to in the relatively small space allotted. I can promise you, however, that your ability to recall names will increase tremendously with the information contained here.

While the techniques of learning to remember names are all here, what is missing is a comprehensive list of audionyms for names. Being prepared is the key to becoming adept at recalling names. Such a project really needs to be approached in greater detail by those motivated to do so.

The only thing that saves most of us from a life of total embarrassment is that most of the population is nearly equally inept when it comes to remembering names. That's very sad. We escape embarrassment simply because hardly anyone else can remember names very well either.

Because the inability to recall names is such a universal failing, those whose names are forgotten by us are, perhaps, less wounded than they might be if nearly everyone were superbly talented in recalling names. But even in a world where people do not remember names very well, nobody ever quite likes it when his or her own name is forgotten. A small irritation is an irritation, nevertheless.

Most competitive games are won, not only on the skill of the players, but on the mistakes and lack of skill of the opponents as well. Negatives play as important a part in many sports—and businesses— as do positives. That goes for the small hurts and slights we inflict by forgetting names. The Chinese call this accumulation of affronts the "Death of a thousand razor cuts." It's reasonable to assume that one less negative in our business, social, or academic lives would give us just that much more of an advantage.

It takes relatively little time and effort to learn memory techniques and to apply them to remembering names. It is such an uncommonly applied skill that those who do employ it stand out from all the rest.

If you walk into a party and are introduced to several dozen people throughout the evening, how many are you able to go back to later and recall by name? If you are like most people, the answer is, not very many.

Suppose you were able to go back to an individual, whom you may have met an hour or more earlier, and say something like, "Waldo, I was wondering whether you might be related to the

Pasadena Gumfdormacherheinzes?" To say the very least, that would certainly get his attention. And the chances are pretty good you will not merely have an interesting conversation, but will find yourself standing before a dumbfounded admirer.

You will have impressed the socks off Waldo, and will be forever held in high regard by him and everyone to whom he relates the story. Multiply this effect by not only remembering his name several hours later at a party, but at some future meeting on a street, in a store, or in a business situation weeks, months—even years later: "Well, darned if it isn't Waldo Gumfdormacherheinz. I haven't seen you since Gilmore Xotzenoffer's party in 2001." Do that and you will become a person not to be forgotten yourself. That's memory power.

Everyone can remember names. What we lack is organization and the willingness to invest just a little time to learn how to do it.

To remember someone's name is to show that person that you believe they are important. And that makes you important to them as well. If a person remembers your name, you respond much more positively to them. You are much more likely to return to a place of business where your name is remembered.

Because most of us remember much more of what we see than of what we hear or read, we have to learn to change audible and abstract printed data into objects we can see in our minds. Applying this concept to names, we simply change names that we hear or read into things we can see—objects that can be visualized—or audionyms.

The object we see must sound like or suggest the name to be remembered. For example:

An audionym for Ken could be *can*.
An audionym for Sally could be *salad*.
An audionym for Hu could be *hoop*.

An audionym for Manuel could be *manual*.

An audionym for Habib could be *hairy bib.*

You cannot see a Ken, a Sally, a Hu, a Manuel, or a Habib, but you can see a can, a salad, a hoop, a manual, or a hairy bib.

It is best to have an audionym already in mind for the most common names you are likely to hear. The uncommon names you encounter will be the only ones you will have to spend any time on. The unusual names, by the way, are often the easiest for which to make on-the-spot audionyms. It is also important that you develop audionyms for both first and last names.

Have you ever been in a social situation when someone said something like this, "The guy [or gal] standing near the door is a pilot with ABC Airlines. His [her] name is Myron [Debbie] Beckwith."

Even an hour or so later, you will be able to recall that the person is an airline pilot. You may also remember that he or she flies for ABC Airlines. But will you remember the name? Most likely not. The reason for forgetting the name is as simple as the reason for remembering the occupation.

At the moment it was mentioned that the person was an airline pilot, something happened in your mind. Your imagination automatically and subconsciously went to work. For only an instant, an image—a picture—of an airline pilot flashed through your head. Maybe you even imagined the person seated in the cockpit of a plane.

We all have our idea of what an airline pilot looks like. But what does a Myron (or Debbie) Beckwith look like? This is exactly where our memories become confused.

Engrave this in your mind: *We remember incredibly more of what we see than of what we hear or read.* Therefore, if we want to increase our chances of remembering anything, the best way to do it is to change what we hear or read into mental pictures. So what does a Myron (or Debbie) Beckwith look like? Or a Harlen Grueber? Or a Kimberly Seigleman? The beginning of the answer to that question is: think of an object that sounds like the name you want to remember. Think of an audionym.

Once you have an audionym (a visual soundalike) for the name you want to remember, then associate that audionym with the total person. Make the association illogical. The more illogical the association, the easier it will be to remember.

There is a sequence that must be followed in order for you to be consistently successful in remembering names. Use the following sequence every time you meet someone for the first time:

1. Meet (see) the person and hear the name.
2. Ask the person to repeat his or her name.
3. Change the name into an audionym (a soundalike object).
4. See (imagine) the audionym with the person in an illogical association.
5. See (imagine) the audionym with the person in various activities.

GENERAL RULES

There are certain general rules that you should follow until they become fixed habits. If you observe these rules, your ability to remember names will increase dramatically—even without a memory system!

1. Always ask the person to repeat his or her name. This can be done very politely, in a number of ways:

a. "I'm sorry, I didn't get your name."

b. "Would you mind repeating your first name?"

c. "Sorry, I didn't catch your last name."

d. "I'm sorry, your last name is?"

e. "Would you give me your first name again?"

f. "I'm sorry . . . your last name is—?"

g. "Pardon me, it's Joe . . . ?" (Wait for the last name.)

h. "How do you spell your first name?"

People are flattered to know that you care enough about them to want to remember their names accurately. They don't mind being asked to repeat their name. If you have an unusual name or know someone who has, you can appreciate what a person goes through. Imagine, if you can, a lifetime of getting mail with a badly misspelled name—oddly similar, but frustratingly different from your own. Imagine being called in class by some sound with too many or too few syllables, or with some of the syllables juggled around. Such sufferers are especially appreciative when someone—at long last—cares enough to take the time and the effort to get their name right.

2. During the handshake, always keep a firm grip until the person has repeated his or her name. If you will observe this rule, you will soon develop the habit of always asking for the name to be repeated. The biggest problem with people who don't remember names is that they never even heard it during the introduction.

3. When you meet someone, concentrate on the person you are meeting—rather than wondering what they might be think-

ing of you. If you really want to remember names, then you will find it easy to be interested, not only in the person's name, but in what that person has to say. The most successful students I have ever taught have been those who are sincere, caring people and are honestly interested in the people they meet.

There is no finer act of sincerity than to give the person you are meeting all of your attention. Even if the president of the United States were to walk by at that moment, you should not notice. The most important thing in your life for those moments must be what that person has to say.

4. Enjoy the opportunity to meet and remember people. Let them know that you want to remember their names. Tell them that you are studying the art of remembering names. You will be surprised at the number of people who will give you an easy way to do it—especially if they have a difficult name.

The people who remember names well are usually the ones who become the most popular. There are so few who can do it well that those who can do it are held in high regard. It is said of Napoleon that he knew all of his 10,000 officers by name. President Franklin D. Roosevelt continuously amazed his staff and associates with his remarkable ability to remember their names.

Follow all of the rules of remembering names because they work! Your reward and your excitement will come when you see the system working for you. I promise you it will happen—very soon.

AUDIONYM CARDS

You may want to use three types of cards as an integral part of a system for remembering names:

1. Audionyms for first names.
2. Audionyms for last names.
3. People I know.

The audionym cards for first and last names are extremely valuable. By having a deck of 3-by-5 cards for the audionyms you create, you can measure your progress as your vocabulary of audionyms increases. Psychologically, this is rewarding—especially when you reach the milestones of 100, 200, 300, or 1,000 audionyms that you confidently know. Also, the audionym cards can be used as a set of flash cards to:

1. Look at the name and try to remember the audionym.
2. Look at the audionym and try to remember the name.

The cards can be filed alphabetically by name so you can continue to add newly developed audionyms in an organized manner as you create them.

Few hobbies are as exciting and practical as collecting audionyms for use in remembering names. The audionym cards let you see your collection as it grows. As your file grows, so will your interest and enthusiasm for your new hobby.

The "people I know" cards would include names, addresses, and phone numbers of the people you know and could include where and when you met and any other pertinent information.

The use of the audionym cards will serve as a well-organized system for documentation, practice, reference, and accumulation of data. I urge you to immediately use audionym cards as you begin to learn audionyms for names!

You should always carry some cards with you to record any new audionyms that you develop during the day, to record the pertinent data of the new people you meet, and so you can store the cards in your permanent file when you return home. *The use of audionym cards as outlined above will be the key to your immediate, rapid, and continuing success in this exciting new endeavor. It would be most practical to enter the information into an electronic database on your computer.*

You can remember names if you have a sincere desire to do so. The ability to remember names has to be developed. It will take some effort on your part, but it will be worth it. You will be surprised to discover that your ability to remember names can develop remarkably fast.

One of the secrets to remembering names is that every name must be changed into something you can see—a tangible object. Don't use action words or words descriptive of action. For example, if we were to form an image for the name Harris, one system would have you use the word *harass*. Well, what does a *harass* look like? When trying to recall the word later, we might confuse it with *worry* or *annoy*. One major problem with adjectives and verbs is that they can have many synonyms—words that mean the same thing, but sound different. The object of memory training is to organize our thoughts—not to add to the confusion. I believe that a good audionym for Harris is *hairs*. You can see *hairs* very clearly in your mind. Common sense and our often-underrated natural memory will translate *hairs* to Harris for us.

Some memory systems use a rhyming technique. But, too often, that system breaks down because, even though the word may rhyme with the name, the use of a different sound—especially at the beginning of the word—can cause chaos when you try to change the word back again.

If a name begins with a consonant sound, try to create an audionym that begins with the same consonant sound—or, at least, the same phonetic sound.

You may freely interchange *b*s with *p*s or *f*s with *v*s and *ph*s when creating audionyms. However, whenever possible, always try to begin an audionym with the same letter as the word you want to remember. If you can't find a satisfactory soundalike with the same first letter, then use another (but similar) first letter.

Part of the success of my memory system is its consistency. If a *can* is always the audionym for Ken, then when a can comes to your mind it will always be Ken. If you have some Kens carrying a can, while others carry a cane, and still others are carrying a cone, there will be confusion. When a Ken enters your life, the name will always be represented by a can. There can be no mistaking it, no confusing the object with anything else. Just by adding a single audionym to your visual vocabulary, you add an image that can be used over and over again. Therefore, you will very rapidly develop your ability to remember names.

The most often used technique for remembering names is to pick out some characteristic in the person's face. The problem with that approach is that so many faces have similar characteristics: high foreheads, large noses, small eyes, and on and on. Plus, beards and mustaches can be grown—or shaved off—between one meeting and the next. My approach to remembering names is to use the total person in my image-making. Each person—just like every fingerprint—is different. There are no two people who present exactly the same image. There will be something distinctive about everyone you meet. The important thing is to associate the audionym illogically with the total person. Use only those things that are immediately apparent: the total face or his or her relative build—tall, short, large or small frame, and so on.

There is one exception to the claim that no two people have the same characteristics: twins. It is not actually an exception to the rule, it's an addition to the rule. The principle still applies. Even in the case of identical twins, there are differences that can be detected. My brother Dale and I are identical twins. People who don't know us well often say they can't tell us apart.

I do not depend completely on the total person technique in the case of identical twins. I look for anything I can find to distinguish them and then make that a major part of my audionym association.

HOW TO DEVELOP AUDIONYMS FOR NAMES

The secret to developing audionyms for names is to establish rules and then to always follow them. Again, consistency is important. An audionym must always be a soundalike that you can see. Some names give us a head start:

Baker	Ball	Bell	Burger
Carpenter	Castle	Farmer	Gardner
Glass	Hill	Hooke	Hunter
Judge	Mason	Paine	Painter
Robins	Shoemaker	Showers	Stein
Steppe	Trout	Wood	Wolfe

Your first thought in developing an audionym should be to ask yourself, "Does the name sound like something I can see?" If so, you have an audionym. All of the names in the list above immediately call to mind a mental image. There are hundreds of names such as these for which you will have no difficulty in forming a visual image. You will be amazed at the many hundreds of names that immediately suggest an audionym that's a common object.

If the name does not immediately give you a picture, your second step should be to ask yourself, "Can the name be broken apart to immediately give me pictures of all the parts?" Here are some examples:

Name	Audionym
Appleyard	apple-yard
Archfield	arch-field
Ashcombe	ash-comb
Ashwell	ash-well
Barbush	bar-bush
Barnhart	barn-heart
Bateman	bait-man
Beeman	bee-man

There are thousands of names in these two categories alone.

Your third step should be to ask yourself, "Does any part of the name sound like something that I can see?" Here are some examples of such names:

Name	Audionym
Ambrose	amber-**rose**
Ashmon	**ash**-moon
Ashmore	**ash**-mower
Axtel	**ax**-tel(ephone)
Badman	bat-**man** (T and D can be used interchangably)
Bagdonis	**bag**-doughnuts
Bailor	**bale**-oar

None of the above names immediately bring a visual image to mind. But all of them have a part that is an object you can see. You must develop the ability to create an audionym for the rest of the name in cases like this. My book, *How to Master the Art of Remembering Names*, provides you with a head start of thousands of audionyms already developed.

The fourth type of names simply does not suggest anything to us. The names are not—totally or in part—descriptive of any object. There are common endings, however, that can be visualized and standardized to make them easy to remember. Examples:

Ending	Audionym	Names
-win	windmill	Norwin, Baldwin, Caldwin
-baugh	ball	Stambaugh, Radabaugh, Cavenbaugh
-er	ear	Klinger, Rissinger, Swanger
-per	purse	Culpepper, Klepper, Mumper
-ow	owl	Clow, Row, Stow
-is	ice	Mathis, Curtis, Landis

If your learn audionyms for the word parts, you will be amazed at how easy it will be to have a clear visual image for even the most unusual names. By learning audionyms for standard parts of names, you will rarely be in a position where you cannot immediately come up with a visual image for names you have never even heard before. You should—as part of your memory training—learn to dissect words. Break them down into parts and construct audionyms for each part for later use.

One more suggestion: the next time you are going to a social or business gathering, try to get a list of the names of all the people who will be there. Study that list. Create an audionym for every name on the list. All that remains is to link your soundalike objects with the proper people. I often leave for a meeting thinking, "One of the guys at this meeting will be carrying a huge can, because there is a Ken on the list of guests, and one of the gals will be carrying a gigantic salad because there is a Sally on the list."

It is a tremendous experience to attend a business or social function and be able to remember the names of everybody at the gathering. It certainly is satisfying.

Step 10

HOW TO SPEAK WITHOUT NOTES

Speaking in public is one thing. Speaking confidently without notes is something indeed! Imagine being able to appear before an audience so well prepared that you could speak for a minute to an hour without any notes and never have any concern that you would forget what you want to say or how you want to say it!

The numbered Cube system has made it possible for thousands of individuals to conquer the fear of public speaking and to become very skilled at it. If you ever need to speak in public, give a report or an introduction, or make a sales presentation, the numbered Cube system is likely to become your very best friend. It's like having your own personal prompter with you all the time.

Prepare your speech or presentation just as you normally would. When you have it written, break it apart into individual thoughts of one or two sentences each. Look at the individual thought or sentence and select the one or two words that will trigger the complete sentence for you. After you have selected the main words, convert them to audionyms. Use the Cube system to place the audionym in each of the numbered room locations. You can then *see* your entire speech.

You may have a fear of speaking in public. Most people do. In fact, it is listed as the number one fear, ranking even above the fear of death. I'll share with you the fact that there was a time, many years ago, when I had a fear of speaking in front of anyone—even to give a report to a small group. It was so bad that I would nearly "choke up" on a silent prayer!—just kidding, of course, but it was almost that bad!

Today I am fortunate to have what some believe to be a rare and coveted gift—to be able to deliver a powerful, persuasive, and motivational presentation with absolute confidence and ease. Even better, I always do it without notes, and you can too!

Having delivered many hundreds of keynote speeches for state, national, and international conventions of academic and business leaders (to as many as eight thousand in one audience), I am certain most people think I was born with a natural ability to be a dynamic speaker. The truth is just the opposite! Until my early twenties—when I was beginning to develop my learning system— I always dreaded when it was my turn to give a report or say anything in front of anyone other than my family or friends. The memory system changed that very dramatically. The most dramatic change, however, came when I developed the numbered Cube system.

I don't think it is possible to become a great speaker if you have to read to your audience. No truly great speaker has ever "moved the masses" by simply reading their speech. The numbered Cube system can give you the tools and the confidence you need to deliver your speech or presentation without notes.

Let's look at an outline of a speech I once presented. I have selected this example because the speech included just ten key thoughts. I wrote the middle of the speech first. That is, I developed the ten key thoughts before I wrote the opening and closing remarks.

I titled the speech, "Ten Qualities for Success." This, of course, was a natural for the Cube system. Did you ever notice how many times there are ten of something?

Top ten songs
Top ten movies
Ten best-dressed men or women
Ten most populated countries of the world
Ten most populated U.S. cities
Ten Commandments
Ten dos of public speaking
Ten don'ts of public speaking
Ten qualities for success

Here are the ten qualities for success that I used in my speech:

1. Attitude
2. Memory
3. Organization
4. Motivation
5. Purpose
6. Knowledge
7. Plan
8. Confidence
9. Honesty
10. Goal

When I have just ten things to learn, I use the ceiling as the number ten location (even though it is actually the zero location) because then I can keep all ten items in one room.

In preparing the speech, the first step was to convert what I wanted to remember into something I could see. Here is how I did it:

Topic	Audionym
attitude	attic
memory	mummy
organization	organ
motivation	motor
purpose	porpoise
knowledge	knoll (a small hill)
plan	plant
confidence	confetti
honesty	honor roll
goal	goalpost

The second step was to visualize one audionym in each of the ten room locations of the room I was using for the ten qualities for success. For example, I saw:

1. An **attic** bursting through the back left corner
2. A **mummy** bursting through the left wall
3. An **organ** bursting out of the front left corner
4. A gigantic **motor** bursting out of the front wall
5. A huge **porpoise** leaping out of the front right corner
6. A **knoll** bursting through the right wall
7. A gigantic **plant** bursting out of the back right corner
8. **Confetti** pouring out of the entire back wall
9. A gigantic **honor roll** covering the entire floor
10. A **goalpost** sticking out of the ceiling (as the tenth item, even though the ceiling is normally the zero location)

Your first reaction might be, "Why would you memorize this list of ten items when you could just use notes?" The difference is between making a speech and making an impression; between looking at your notes and looking them in the eye; between looking like an amateur and being a professional.

During the presentation—which was to a large, but rather informal, sales group—when I was talking about organization someone asked if planning was part of organization. Because I was talking about organization (*organ* to me), I knew I was at the front left corner in my room. I knew that planning (*plant* to me), was in the back right corner. So I said, "I'll be covering planning as a separate quality. I have three more items to cover after organization and then we'll cover planning."

All of a sudden, there was a spontaneous applause. It sort of caught me off guard, but I quickly realized by the audience feedback—including one thumbs-up—that I had just demonstrated the power of my system. Even with the interruption, I was able to answer the question and let him know I had three more topics to cover after organization before I would get to planning. Then I mentally returned to the front left corner, saw the *organ,* and continued to talk about organization.

You can now see how to present a speech without notes. Just create the outline, then create audionyms for each subject and place them in sequence around the room or rooms. You are likely to already know what you want to say about each subject. If you don't, just create audionyms for more of the words in the presentation. You will discover, however, that only one or two audionyms for each thought will be enough to enable you to discuss in your own words what you want to say about each subject.

An alternate method for remembering the above topics for a speech is to link the audionyms instead of using the Cube method. The Cube method works best, however, because it offers the opportunity to link the subtopics starting with the audionym in each of the numbered Cube locations.

Part II

MORE PRACTICAL APPLICATIONS

From this point on in the book, I will show you actual applications of my system applied to numerous subjects. Just by reading and understanding how the system can be applied to a wide range of subjects, you will understand how to apply the system to many of your specific needs.

REMEMBER THE TEN STEPS TO MEMORY POWER IN THIS BOOK

I was enjoying breakfast with my twin brother, Dale, about an hour ago. I was nearing completion of this book, and I reviewed with him the contents. When I told him about the section on remembering the contents of a book, he asked if I had included any examples of an actual book or if I had just included the system for doing it. I told him that I had not included any specific examples because the reader would understand how to do it just by an explanation of the system. He agreed, but still suggested that I take advantage of the opportunity to apply the system to this book. "After all," he said, "your book teaches the reader how to learn the contents of any other book. To remember the contents of your book is to remember all the tools one needs to remember anything." That makes sense—I should have thought of it myself!

Dale made another interesting point: "Most books for which you would want to recall its contents have a theme and a chronology. This book, because of necessity, includes chapters with unrelated subjects. Readers will understand that when the system works for this book, it will work for any book."

Following is an actual example of the system applied to an outline of an entire book—*this book*. It will automatically give you a way to remember all the techniques and tools to remember anything. It will also enable you to mentally review this entire book at any time.

First, select a familiar room. At the ceiling, see this book, but it is a gigantic book stuck in the ceiling! Anytime you want to review the contents of this book, just think of a gigantic copy of this book stuck in the ceiling of the room you selected.

To recall what is taught in Step 1, think of location 1—the back left corner of the room. Step 1 teaches the numbered Cube. Look at location 1 and see a gigantic Cube! Later, when you think of location 1—the back left corner—the Cube will enable you to remember that Step 1 teaches the numbered Cube. You already know that the Cube is numbered from zero through nine or ten through nineteen, etc.

For Step 2, think of location 2—the left wall. Step 2 teaches the audionym technique. Change audionym to *audio system* and see the left wall with gigantic speakers blasting music out of the center of the wall! Later, when you think of location 2—the left wall—the audio speakers will remind you that Step 2 teaches the audionym technique. You already know that an audionym is a soundalike object you can see and that it represents the word you want to remember.

For Step 3, think of location 3—the front left corner. Step 3 teaches the association technique. Change association to an audionym—a *seashell*. See a gigantic seashell bursting out of the front left corner of the room! Later, when you think of location 3—the front left corner—the seashell will remind you that Step 3 teaches the association technique.

You already know that the association technique always involves only two objects at a time: one object represents what you already know and the other object represents what you want to remember.

Though they are usually two common objects, they are associated together in some illogical way. It is important to always start with the object that represents what you already know and associate with it the audionym representing what you want to remember.

For Step 4, think of location 4—the front wall. Step 4 teaches the Link system. Change Link to an audionym—*links* (a bracelet). See links bursting out of the front wall of the room! Later, when you think of location 4—the front wall—the links will remind you that Step 4 teaches the Link system. You already know that the Link system is repeated associations of audionyms linked together with each new audionym becoming the audionym you already know, to which you link the next new audionym.

For Step 5, think of location 5—the front right corner. Step 5 teaches the Number Code. Change Number Code to an audionym—*numbers*. See numbers pouring out of the front right corner of the room! Later, when you think of location 5—the front right corner—the numbers will remind you that Step 5 teaches the Number Code system. You already know that the Number Code involves converting numbers to consonant letters of the alphabet and that the vowels and w, h, and y have no number value. You also know that double consonants represent a single sound. You know, too, that words are converted to numbers based on sound, not on how the words are spelled. If you can't hear the consonant you don't convert it to a number.

For Step 6, think of location 6—the right wall. Step 6 teaches the Key Word system. Change Key Word to an audionym—*keyboard*. See a gigantic keyboard stuck into the right wall of the room! Later, when you think of location 6—the right wall—the keyboard will remind you that Step 6 teaches the Key Word system.

You already know that the Key Word system is a set of one hundred words for the numbers zero-zero through ninety-nine.

There are also Key Words for the single-digit numbers (zero through nine). The Key Words are the words you always think of first for any number from zero to ninety-nine.

For Step 7, think of location 7—the right wall. Step 7 teaches the Topograph system. Change Topograph to an audionym—*top* (a child's toy top). See a gigantic child's top spinning at the right wall of the room! Later, when you think of location 7—the right wall—the top will remind you that Step 7 teaches the Topograph system.

You already know that the Topograph system is used to remember parts of a whole, such as the bones of the body, countries of a continent, or parts of an engine or a piece of equipment. It is used both to recall all the parts of a whole and the relative size and location of each part in relation to the other parts or to the whole.

For Step 8, think of location 8—the back wall. Step 8 teaches the Grid system. Change Grid to an audionym—*griddle*. See a gigantic griddle at the back right corner of the room! Later, when you think of location 8—the back wall—the griddle will remind you that Step 8 teaches the Grid system.

You already know that the Grid system is actually a memory bank of objects (audionyms). The audionyms are created by using the equivalent of a checkerboard with any number of squares. The rows are lettered down the left side of the grid. The columns are numbered across the top of the grid. An audionym is created from the intersection of each letter and number (location B1 could have any of the following audionyms: **b**oat, **b**eet, **b**oot, **b**ait, **b**at, **b**it, **b**utt, or **b**ooth. The grid locations can serve as the equivalent of the numbered Cube because you can easily find any location sequentially or randomly.

For Step 9, think of location nine—the floor. Step 9 teaches you how to remember names. Change Names to an audionym—*names*. See thousands of names written all over the floor of the room! Later, when you think of location 9—the floor—the names will remind you that Step 9 teaches you how to remember names.

You already know that every name can be changed to an audionym and that you associate the audionym with the total person. By building a vocabulary of audionyms for male and female first names, as well as last names, the art of remembering names becomes easier every day. It is best to review the rules for developing audionyms for names. It includes many standards for names and parts of names, such as common endings.

For Step 10, think of location 10—the ceiling. Step 10 teaches you how to speak without notes. Change Speak to an audionym—*speaker*. See a gigantic speaker on the ceiling of the room! Later, when you think of location 10—the ceiling—the speaker will remind you that Step 10 teaches you how to speak without notes.

You now know the ten steps to a powerful memory covered in this book. There are thousands of applications of these ten steps, especially when they are used in combination with each other. By knowing the ten steps, you have *ten* memory tools that can be used in various combinations to remember virtually anything!

DEPARTMENTS OF GOVERNMENT

Following are audionyms representing the names of the departments in the President's cabinet. Here are the names of the fifteen current departments of the cabinet:

Department	Audionym or Picture
Agriculture	agreement (contract)
Commerce	comic book
Defense	deer-fence (a deer on a fence)
Education	edger (for trimming lawns)
Energy	energy bar (nutritional)
Health and Human Services	heel
Homeland Security	home
Housing and Urban Development	housing development
Interior	interior decorator
Justice	juice
Labor	label
State	state police
Transportation	trains

Department	Audionym or Picture
Treasury	treasure chest
Veterans Affairs	veteran

To remember the names of the departments (in alphabetical order), just start with the first one (location 1). See a gigantic **agreement** (**Agriculture**) in location 1—the back left corner of your Units room. Continue around to the floor (location 9). Then visualize your 10s room where you will place the pictures or audionyms around to location 15. Recall the audionyms and they will remind you of the name of each department in the President's cabinet.

THE BILL OF RIGHTS

As part of the legislation requiring schools to teach information about the Constitution, I had the opportunity to teach the Bill of Rights to hundreds of sixth, seventh, and eighth graders in a Winston-Salem, North Carolina, elementary school. It was a thrill to have students come to the front of the auditorium and accurately recall the ten amendments, including, for example, the five rights granted in the first amendment alone.

The Bill of Rights, the first ten amendments to the Constitution, can be learned in ten to fifteen minutes using the memory tools you have learned so far. Even if you are not interested in this information, please complete at least the first two or three amendments so you know how the system works.

1. Read each amendment. (I have highlighted the most important points.)

2. Use the Cube starting with location 1 (because it is important to know the amendments by their number).

3. Place the first audionym for each amendment in the numbered Cube location for that amendment. Then link the rest of the audionyms for the amendment.

AMENDMENT I

"Congress shall make no law respecting an establishment of **religion,** or prohibiting the free exercise thereof; or abridging the freedom of **speech,** or of the **press;** or the right of the people peaceably to **assemble,** and to **petition** the Government for a redress of grievances."

Right	Audionym
religion	reel
speech	spatula
press	pretzel
peaceful assembly	assembly
petition	pet

In location 1 see a gigantic **reel (religion)!**
The reel is reeling in a **spatula (speech)!**
The spatula has a **pretzel** on it **(press)!**
The pretzel has an **assembly** on it **(assembly)!**
Everyone in the assembly is holding a **pet (petition)!**
When you visualize location 1, you should see **reel, spatula, pretzel, assembly,** and **pets**. This will remind you of **religion, speech, press, assembly, petition,** the five rights included in the first amendment.

AMENDMENT II

"A well regulated Militia being necessary to the security of a free State, the right of the people to **keep and bear arms,** shall not be infringed."

Right	Audionym
keep and bear arms	arms

Look at location 2 and see gigantic **arms (keep and bear arms)** sticking out of the wall!

Later, just glancing at the left wall mentally and seeing the **arms** will remind you of the second amendment guaranteeing the right to **keep and bear arms.**

AMENDMENT III

"No **soldier** shall, in time of peace, be **quartered** in any house, without the consent of the owner, nor in time of war, but in a manner to be prescribed by law."

Right	Audionym
quartering of soldiers	quarter-soldiers

Look at location 3 and see a gigantic **quarter with soldiers** on it!

Later, just glancing at the front left corner and visualizing the **quarter with soldiers** will remind you of the third amendment prohibiting the **quartering of soldiers** without the consent of the owner.

AMENDMENT IV

"The right of the people to be secure in their persons, houses, papers, and effects, against **unreasonable searches and seizures,** shall not be violated, and no Warrants shall issue, but upon probable cause, supported by Oath or affirmation, and particularly describing the place to be searched and the persons or things to be seized."

Right	**Audionym**
unreasonable search and seizure	searchlight

Look at location 4 and see a gigantic **searchlight** on it!

Later, just glancing at the front wall and visualizing the **searchlight** will remind you of the fourth amendment prohibiting **unreasonable searches and seizures.**

AMENDMENT V

"No person shall be held to answer for a capital, or otherwise infamous crime, unless on a presentment or indictment of a **Grand Jury,** except in cases arising in the land or naval forces, or in the Militia, when in actual service in time of War or public danger; nor shall any person be subject for the same offence to be **twice put in jeopardy** of life or limb; nor shall be compelled in any criminal case to be a **witness against himself,** nor be deprived of life, liberty, or property, without due process of law; nor shall **private property** be taken for public use, without just compensation."

Right	Audionym
Grand Jury	grandstand
double jeopardy	double-decker
self-witness	shelf-white nest
(private) property	propeller

Look at location 5 and see a **grandstand (Grand Jury)**!

The grandstand has a **double-decker** bus in it! **(double jeopardy)**

The double-decker bus has a **shelf** with a **white nest** on it! **(shelf-white nest-self-witness)**

The shelf with a white nest on it has a **propeller** on it! **(private property)**

Later, just glancing at the front right corner and visualizing the **grandstand, double-decker, shelf-white nest,** and **propeller** will remind you of the fifth amendment, which addresses **Grand Jury, double jeopardy, self-witness,** and **private property.**

AMENDMENT VI

"In all criminal prosecutions, the accused shall enjoy the right to a **speedy and public trial,** by an impartial jury of the State and district wherein the crime shall have been committed, which district shall have been previously ascertained by law, and to be informed of the nature and cause of the accusation; to be confronted with the witnesses against him; to have compulsory process for obtaining witnesses in his favor, and to have the Assistance of Counsel for his defense."

Right	Audionym
speedy trial	speed limit sign

Look at location 6 and see a gigantic **speed limit sign**!

Later, just glancing at the right wall and visualizing the **speed limit sign** will remind you of the sixth amendment assuring a **speedy trial.**

AMENDMENT VII

"In Suits at common law, where the value in controversy shall exceed twenty dollars, the right of **trial by jury** shall be preserved, and no fact tried by a jury, shall be otherwise reexamined in any Court of the United States, than according to the rules of the common law."

Right	Audionym
trial by jury	jury box

Look at location 7 and see a **jury box**!

Later, just glancing at the back right corner and visualizing the **jury** will remind you of the seventh amendment assuring the right of trial by jury.

AMENDMENT VIII

"**Excessive bail** shall not be required, nor excessive fines imposed, nor **cruel and unusual punishments** inflicted."

Right	Audionym
excessive bail	bale (of hay)
cruel and unusual punishments	punch (bowl)

Look at location 8 and see a **bale** of hay! The bale has a **punch** (bowl) on it!

Later, just glancing at the front wall and visualizing the **bale** of hay and the **punch** (bowl) will remind you of the eighth amendment prohibiting **excessive bail** or **cruel and unusual punishments.**

AMENDMENT IX

"The enumeration in the Constitution, of certain **rights,** shall not be construed to deny or disparage those retained by the **people.**"

Right	**Audionym**
peoples' rights	people

Look at location 9 and see **people** all over the floor!

Later, just glancing at the floor and visualizing the **people** will remind you of the ninth amendment protecting **people's** rights.

AMENDMENT X

"The powers not delegated to the United States by the Constitution, nor prohibited by it to the **States,** are reserved to the States respectively, or to the people."

Right	**Audionym**
States' rights	states

Look at location 10 and see a gigantic map of the United **States** on it!

Later, just "glancing" at the ceiling and visualizing the **states** will remind you of the tenth amendment reserving **States' rights.**

REVIEW

Amendment	Audionym	Right
I	reel	religion
	spatula	speech
	pretzel	press
	assembly	assemble
	pets	petition
II	arms	keep and bear arms
III	quarter with soldiers	quartering soldiers
IV	searchlight	unreasonable searchcs and seizures
V	grandstand	Grand Jury
	double-decker	double jeopardy
	shelf-white nest	self-witness
	propeller	(private) property
VI	speed limit sign	speedy trial
VII	jury box	trial by jury
VIII	bale (of hay)	excessive bail
	punch (bowl)	cruel and unusual punishment
IX	people	peoples' rights
X	states	States' rights

HOW TO REMEMBER THE SIGNS
AND DATES OF THE ZODIAC

To remember the signs of the zodiac, start by changing the name of each sign to an audionym.

Zodiac Sign	**Audionym**
Aquarius	aquarium

Pisces	pies

Zodiac Sign	Audionym
Aries	airplane

| Taurus | tar |

| Gemini | gem |

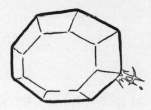

| Cancer | can |

Zodiac Sign	Audionym
Leo	leaf

Virgo	fur coat

Libra	library

Scorpio	scoreboard

Zodiac Sign	Audionym
Sagittarius	satchel

Capricorn	cap

Since there are twelve months and twelve signs, we'll place the audionym for each month at its numbered location on the clock.

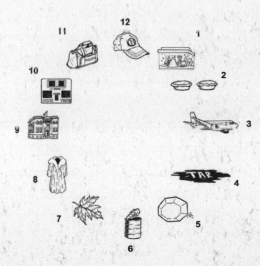

1. January: aquarium, Aquarius
2. February: pies, Pisces
3. March: airplane, Aries
4. April: tar, Taurus
5. May: gem, Gemini
6. June: can, Cancer
7. July: leaf, Leo
8. August: fur coat, Virgo
9. September: library, Libra
10. October: scoreboard, Scorpio
11. November: satchel, Sagittarius
12. December: cap, Capricorn

By remembering the location of the audionyms on the clock, you can remember to which month each sign belongs.

All the dates of the signs begin between the nineteenth and the twenty-third of the month, so there is no need for a system to remember the first digit of the date. Each of the numbers nine (for the nineteenth) and zero through three (for the twentieth through the twenty-third) is changed to an audionym.

19. Nine is changed to *knife*
20. Zero is changed to *cereal*
21. One is changed to *wand*
22. Two is changed to *tuba*
23. Three is changed to *tree*

You don't have to memorize the date a sign ends, because it always ends on the day before the next sign begins.

Each of the audionyms will have either cereal, a wand, a tuba, or a tree associated with it to tell you the date on which the sign begins. You already know the month on which each sign begins by knowing where its audionym is located on the clock.

January: see the **aquarium** with **cereal** in it! (**Aquarius: cereal, 0, 20**)

February: see the **pies** with a **knife** stuck through them! (**Pisces: knife, 9, 19**)

March: see the **airplane** with a gigantic **wand** on it! (**Aries: wand, 1, 21**)

April: see the **tar** with **cereal** in it! (**Taurus: cereal, 1, 20**)

May: see the **gem** with a **wand** on it! (**Gemini: wand, 1, 21**)

June: see the **can** with a **wand** in it! (**Cancer: wand, 1, 21**)

July: see the **leaf** with a **tree** in it! (**Leo: tree, 3, 23**)

August: see the **fur coat** with a **tree** in it! (**Virgo: tree, 3,** 23)

September: see the **library** with a **tree** stuck in it! (**Libra: tree, 3,** 23)

October: see the **scoreboard** with a **tree** stuck in it! (**Scorpio: tree, 3,** 23)

November: see the **satchel** with a **tuba** in it! (**Sagittarius: tuba, 2, 22**)

December: see the **cap** with a **tuba** in it! (**Capricorn: tuba, 2, 22**)

I recognize there are different opinions about the precise date on which some of the signs begin. It's easy to change the associations to adjust to the dates you use if they are different than those indicated here. You now have a simple method for determining, not only the month, but the day of the month on which each sign begins.

HOW TO REMEMBER
WHERE YOU PUT THINGS

How many times have you said, "I can't find my keys / glasses / new pen / cell phone"? How much time have you spent looking for things you've misplaced? Finally, there is a way to remember where you put things. For each item you put somewhere, it will take about two seconds to lock it in your mind so you'll know where it is when you need it.

I am going to place five common items in different locations and use a simple, organized system to show you how to remember where each item is placed.

Let's start with your sunglasses. You place your sunglasses in a drawer in your bedroom. As you place your sunglasses in the drawer, stop just for a second, look at the sunglasses and imagine a gigantic drawer being pulled out of the sunglasses (out through the lens). Think to yourself, sunglasses—see the drawer being pulled out through the lens—drawer. Later, when you think, "Sunglasses," you'll remember the drawer being pulled out of the lens and remember that the sunglasses are in the drawer.

You place your car keys under a pillow on the sofa. As you place your keys under the pillow, stop just for a second, look at the keys and imagine using the pillow instead of your keys to unlock and start your car! Think to yourself, car keys—see yourself using the pillow to unlock and start your car—pillow. Later, when you think, "Car keys," you'll remember trying to unlock and start your car with the pillow and remember that the car keys are under the pillow.

You place your new pen under a desk lamp. As you place your new pen under the desk lamp, stop just for a second, look at the new and imagine it with a lamp shade on it (the same lamp shade on the lamp under which you place the new pen). Think to yourself, new pen—imagine the new pen with the lamp shade on it—lamp shade. Later, when you think, "New pen," you'll remember the new pen with the lamp shade on it and remember that the new pen is under the lamp.

You place your gloves in a pair of shoes you seldom wear. As you place your gloves in the shoes, stop just for a second, look at the gloves and imagine wearing the shoes on your hands instead of the gloves. Think to yourself, gloves—imagine wearing the shoes instead of the gloves—shoes. Later, when you think, "Gloves," you'll remember wearing shoes for gloves and recall that you put your gloves in the shoes.

You place your new credit card in an empty water glass (until you have time to put it in your purse or wallet). As you place your new credit card in the glass, stop just for a second, look at the credit card, and imagine paying for everything with the glass instead of your credit card. Think to yourself, credit card—imagine using a glass for a credit card—glass. Later, when you think, "Credit card," you'll remember using the glass as a credit card and recall that you placed your new credit card in the empty water glass. You'll naturally recall where the glass is located.

Now, recall where you put each of these items: new pen, car keys, credit card, sunglasses, gloves.

The concept of "a place for everything and everything in its place" has a lot of merit. The idea here is that when you put anything anywhere that is *not* in its normal place, stop for a second or two and create a simple, illogical association between the item you place and where you place it. Compare the couple of seconds it will take to mentally store where you put the item to the many minutes or hours you may spend looking for it if you don't do it! The habit is good; the system works and it saves a lot of time.

PRACTICE

Using the same method, look at each item that follows and Where You Put It. Create an association for each of them. Then, cover the Where You Put It column. Look at each item and recall where you put it. Uncover to check your answers.

Item	Where You Put It
special ring	in a glass jar in the kitchen pantry
black leather belt	top shelf in bedroom closet
letter to be mailed to a friend	inside kitchen cabinet with drinking glasses
postage stamps	top of refrigerator
digital camera	behind clock in bedroom
twelve-inch ruler	on shelf in entryway closet
chewing gum	in a cup in the kitchen cabinet
magnifying glass	in cabinet under the TV
flashlight	under the kitchen sink
calculator	behind telephone on nightstand in bedroom

HOW TO REMEMBER
YOUR SCHEDULE AND THINGS TO DO

A simple and easy way to remember your schedule and things to do is to use the numbered Cube. I use different rooms for my schedule than the ones I use for my mental to-do list.

Let's start with a to-do list. Visualize a familiar room. Each to-do item must be converted to something you can see. Let's suggest that you must get your car inspected. You could just visualize your car in location 1 of the room you are using for your to-do list. Imagine your car bursting out of location 1 of the to-do room.

Number 1 has no significance, other than it just happens to be the first item you placed on the list. The next item would be placed at the next location—the left wall.

If the next thing on the list is to pick up items at the dry cleaner, just imagine the next location in your to-do room and imagine dry-cleaning items piled from the floor to the ceiling at that location.

With this system, you can start with an initial list and add to it at any time. When you complete an item in a room location, you can replace it with another item. For example, if you want to add another item to the to-do list, such as sending a thank you card to a friend, and you already had your car inspected, you can just replace the car with a gigantic thank you card in the same location. So, instead of seeing the car at the back left corner of the to-do room, you now see a gigantic thank you card bursting out of the corner.

If you have not yet picked up the dry cleaning, it will still be stacked up at the left wall. It is easy to review ten items in the to-do list in just one room. If you need more than ten items at a time, use additional rooms.

The system you use for remembering your schedule depends on how busy your schedule is. Some people use one room for each day of the week. Others can get by with a single room. I use seven rooms for the seven days of the week.

The system is identical to the to-do room described earlier, except that I add (using the Number Code) the time of day, if that is necessary. Here is an example: if I have an appointment on Wednesday, I use my Wednesday room. If the appointment is at 9:45 A.M. I use the Code Word *pearl* (which converts to 945 with the Number Code). Natural memory is sufficient to know if it is A.M. or P.M.

I just link the *pearl* to the object I use for the appointment itself. If I later add another appointment that is earlier than 9:45 A.M. I put it in the next available room location, even though it is to occur earlier than the item in the location before it. It is so easy to mentally scan the appointments for the day that it does not make any difference in which sequence they occur in the room.

When you start using the Cube for to-do things and for your schedule, you will want to keep using it because it is quick and efficient. It is also great for mental exercise. It is just one of many mental activities that will help keep you mentally alert for a lifetime.

STATES AND THE DATES
THEY ENTERED THE UNION

Here is a handy application for practice and a great history lesson. I suggest that you learn all the states first, then start over and add the dates they entered the Union. You will then know the date in which each state entered the Union, because the second object will give you the actual year.

Start with location 1—the back left corner of your Units room.

1. At location 1, see a **deli (Delaware)** with a gigantic **fig (1787)** in it!

2. At location 2, see a **pencil (Pennsylvania)** with a gigantic **fig (1787)** on it!

3. At location 3, see a **new (football) jersey (New Jersey)** with a huge **fig (1787)** on it!

4. At location 4, see **George Washington (Georgia)** playing a **fife (1788)**!

5. At location 5, see a **cone (Connecticut)** with a gigantic **fife** (1788) stuck in it!

6. At location 6, see a **mast (Massachusetts)** of a ship with a gigantic **fife** (1788) stuck through it!

7. At location 7, see **Mary's lamb (Maryland)** with a gigantic **fife** (1788)!

8. At location 8, see **southern carolers (South Carolina)** holding a gigantic **fife** (1788)!

9. At location 9, see a **new ham (New Hampshire)** with a gigantic **fife** (1788) stuck in it!

10s Room

10. At location 10, see a gigantic **Virginia ham (Virginia)** with a huge **fife** (1788) stuck in it!

11. At location 11, see a **new yacht (New York)** with a gigantic **fife** (1788) on it!

12. At location 12, see **northern carolers (North Carolina)** holding a gigantic **fob** (1789)!

13. At location 13, see a **road (Rhode Island)** with a gigantic **bus** (1790) on it!

14. At location 14, see a **fur mountie (Vermont)** holding a gigantic **bat** (1791)!

15. At location 15, see **King Tut (Kentucky)** holding a gigantic **bone** (17**92**)!

16. At location 16, see a gigantic **tennis ball (Tennessee)** with a **beach** (17**96**) on it!

17. At location 17, see an **old hide (Ohio)** with a **sumo wrestler** (18**03**) on it!

18. At location 18, see a gigantic pile of **lace (Louisiana)** with a gigantic **tuna** (18**12**) on it!

19. At location 19, see an **Indian (Indiana)** holding a gigantic **dish** (18**16**)!

20s Room

20. At location 20, see **Miss America (Mississippi)** holding a gigantic **tack** (18**17**)!

21. At location 21, see an **eel (Illinois)** holding a gigantic **TV** (18**18**)!

22. At location 22, see an **album (Alabama)** with a gigantic **top** (18**19**) on it!

23. At location 23, see a **mane (Maine)** with a gigantic **nose** (18**20**) on it!

24. At location 24, see a **moose (Missouri)** with a **net** (18**21**) on it!

25. At location 25, see a gigantic **ark (Arkansas)** with a gigantic **match (1836)** in it!

26. At location 26, see a **machine gun (Michigan)** with a **mug (1837)** coming out of it!

27. At location 27, see a **flower (Florida)** with a **reel (1845)** on it!

28. At location 28, see a gigantic **tack (Texas)** with a **reel (1845)** on it!

29. At location 29, see a gigantic **eye (Iowa)** with a **roach (1846)** on it!

30s Room

30. At location 30, see a gigantic bottle of **whiskey (Wisconsin)** with a **roof (1848)** over it!

31. At location 31, see a gigantic **calendar (California)** with **lace (1850)** around it!

32. At location 32, see a gigantic **minnow (Minnesota)** with a **loaf (1858)** on it!

33. At location 33, see an **organ (Oregon)** with a gigantic **lip (1859)** on it!

34. At location 34, see a gigantic **can (Kansas)** with a **sheet (1861)** over it!

35. At location 35, see a gigantic **Western hat (West Virginia)** with **jam** (18**63**) all over it!

36. At location 36, see a **new father (Nevada)** holding a gigantic **cherry** (18**64**) instead of a baby!

37. At location 37, see a gigantic **new brass key (Nebraska)** with **chalk** (18**67**) on it!

38. At location 38, see a gigantic **collar (Colorado)** with **cash** (18**76**) in it!

39. At location 39, see a **north day coat** (parka) **(North Dakota)** with a gigantic **fob** (18**89**) on it!

40s Room

40. At location 40, see a **south day coat** (swimsuit) **(South Dakota)** with a gigantic **fob** (18**89**) on it!

41. At location 41, see a **mountain (Montana)** with a gigantic **fob** (18**89**) on it!

42. At location 42, see a **washing machine (Washington)** with a gigantic **fob** (18**89**) on it!

43. At location 43, see an **eye doctor (Idaho)** holding a **bus** (18**90**)!

44. At location 44, see a **wire O (Wyoming)** with a gigantic **bus** (18**90**) driving through it!

45. At location 45, see a **U doll (Utah)** holding a gigantic **peach** (18**96**)!

46. At location 46, see an **oak tree (Oklahoma)** with a gigantic **sock** (19**07**) on it!

47. At location 47, see a gigantic **new mixer (New Mexico)** with a **tuna** (19**12**) on it!

48. At location 48, see gigantic **arrows (Arizona)** with a **tuna** (19**12**) riding on them!

49. At location 49, see an **owl with a lasso (Alaska).** The **owl** is lassoing a huge **Lab** (Labrador retriever) (19**59**)!

50s Room

50. At location 50, see a gigantic container of **Hawaiian Punch (Hawaii)** with a **Lab** (Labrador retriever) (19**59**) in it!

If you completed this exercise, you will be able to think of any state and know the numbered sequence in which it entered the Union, as well as its year of entry. This exercise provides an opportunity to practice five of the steps taught in this book: the numbered Cube, the audionym, association, the Number Code, and the Link. Even if you are not interested in the specific information, this system can be used for countless applications.

HOW TO REMEMBER PLAYING CARDS

Every playing card can be changed to a Code Word that is a picture you can see. The first consonant of the Code Word represents the number of the card (ace through ten) or the name of the card, **j** (**j**ack), **q** (**q**ueen). The second consonant represents the name of the suit, **c** (**c**lub), **r** (hea**r**t), **d** (**d**iamond), **s** (**s**pade). Think of the word *cards* to recall the suits in the same sequence.

For the first ten cards in each suit (ace through ten), we'll convert the numbers one through zero to consonants, using the Number Code. These consonants will be used as the first consonant of each Code Word for the first ten cards in each suit as shown below. The second consonant will represent the suit as shown below.

Club	Heart	Diamond	Spade
1 **t**a**ck**	1 **t**i**r**e	1 **t**oa**d**	1 **t**oe**s**
2 **n**e**ck**	2 **n**ew o**ar**	2 **n**ee**d**le	2 **n**o**s**e
3 **m**i**ke**	3 **m**owe**r**	3 **m**u**d**	3 **m**oo**s**e
4 **r**o**ck**	4 **r**owe**r**	4 **r**oa**d**	4 **r**o**s**e
5 **l**o**ck**	5 **l**u**r**e	5 **l**oa**d**	5 **l**a**ss**o
6 **ch**e**ck**	6 **ch**ai**r**	6 **ch**e**dd**ar	6 **ch**e**ss**
7 **c**o**c**oa	7 **c**a**r**	7 **c**o**d**	7 **c**a**s**e

Club	Heart	Diamond	Spade
8 factory	8 fire	8 food	8 fuse
9 package	9 pear	9 poodle	9 peas
10 sack	10 sewer	10 soda	10 sauce
J jack	J jar	J jade	J juice
Q quack	Q quarry	Q quad	Q quiz
K club	K king	K diamond	K spade

After you know the Code Words for all fifty-two cards, mentally review them by suit (all the clubs, then all the hearts, and so on) in sequence. For efficiency, always review the suits in the same order (clubs, hearts, diamonds, spades), using the word *cards* to help you remember the sequence.

To practice remembering which cards have been played (or not played) in a game, when you see a card, quickly change it to its Code Word, then change the picture in some dramatic way (usually by imagining it broken or destroyed).

It is easy to review all the Code Words in sequence in a suit and immediately recall if you had changed it in some manner. If it was changed, the card was played. If it was not changed, the card was not played. As an illustration, we'll use the suit of hearts. Look below at each Card Being Played and What to Do. Remember what is done to each object:

Card Being Played	What to Do
9H (9 of hearts)	Quickly change the 9 of hearts to its Code Word (pear). Imagine the pear being smashed!
JH	Quickly change the Jack of hearts to its Code Word (jar). Imagine the jar being smashed!

Card Being Played	What to Do
6H	Quickly change the 6 of hearts to its Code Word (**ch**a**ir**). Imagine the chair being smashed!
AH	Quickly change the Ace of hearts to its Code Word (**tir**e). Imagine the tire being flat!
7H	Quickly change the 7 of hearts to its Code Word (**car**). Imagine the car being smashed!
2H	Quickly change the 2 of hearts to its Code Word (**n**ew **oar**). Imagine the new oar being broken in half!
KH	Quickly change the King of hearts to its Code Word (**k**ing). Imagine the king's crown being smashed!
8H	Quickly change the 8 of hearts to its Code Word (**fir**e). Imagine the fire with water being poured on it!
10H	Quickly change the 10 of hearts to its Code Word (**s**ewe**r**). Imagine a sewer pipe being bent in half!
3H	Quickly change the 3 of hearts to its Code Word (**m**owe**r**). Imagine the mower being broken in half!

You have now seen ten of the thirteen cards in the suit of hearts. To determine which cards have *not* been played, just review the thirteen Code Words for the suit of hearts in sequence. If the Code Word object was changed in any way, the card was played. If the Code Word object was not changed, the card was not played. Although you would review the Code Words mentally, for this exercise, I'll list them in sequence since you can't be expected to know them yet:

Code Word	Was This Object Changed?	
	Yes	No
tire		
new oar		
mower		
rower		
lure		
chair		
car		
fire		
pear		
sewer		
jar		
quarry		
king		

Ten cards were played. Three were not played. Simply by reviewing all the Code Words for the suit of hearts, you can easily determine which objects were not changed. In the list above, only *rower, lure,* and *quarry* were not changed. This means that 4H, 5H, and QH were not played.

To be efficient, you must be able to review the Code Words for the four suits of cards very rapidly. You will be amazed at how quickly you will be able to review all fifty-two cards when you are just reviewing the Code Words. When reviewing the Code Words, there is no need to convert the words to the names of the cards. That can be done only when you need it.

You can practice with a deck of fifty-two cards after you know all the Code Words. I sometimes shuffle a deck of cards and place five cards facedown. I look at each card and quickly convert it to its Code Word and change it in some way (usually by imagining it smashed or broken).

After looking at all the cards and imagining each object smashed or broken, I use the word *cards* (representing the four suits) to review all the Code Words in each suit (c, r, d, s). When I come to a card and see an object that was not changed (smashed or broken), I know that is one of the five cards that was not played (and is facedown). I make a note of the five cards that are facedown. When I complete the mental review of the fifty-two cards, I turn the five cards over to confirm that I was right. Do I ever miss any? Sure, but not very often, and only if I try to do it too quickly.

Another great mental exercise is to shuffle a deck of cards, turn the cards facedown one at a time. As you look at each card, change it to its Code Word and visualize the object in its numbered room location. You need six rooms to do this, but the sixth room includes only the numbers 50, 51, and 52.

After you look at all fifty-two cards, start at location 1 (the back left corner of the first room) and recall the object in each of the fifty-two numbered room locations. Convert the object in each location to the name of the playing card it represents.

This exercise will truly amaze your family and friends. I suggest that you start with just ten or twenty cards. Each time you do it you may wish to do an additional five or ten cards.

HOW TO REMEMBER WHAT YOU READ

Did you ever get to the bottom of a page and wonder what you just read? That is a very common problem among students and adults. Many people ask, "How can I remember what I read?"

It is not practical to try to remember every word you read. It is practical to read until you find something you want to remember and then use an organized memory system to remember it. When reading information, some of which you want to remember, use the Cube. Select a familiar room. When you read something you want to remember, stop briefly and highlight it or write it down. Then convert the information to audionyms. Associate the audionym(s) with location 1, 2, 3, and so on, in the familiar room. After you have mentally stored nine items of information in the first room, mentally go to the next room and start at the ceiling (location 10) and continue.

After you complete what you are reading, mentally review each numbered room location to recall all of the information you have read. This is an excellent mental exercise and a very practical application of the memory system.

HOW TO REMEMBER
THE CHAPTER OUTLINE OF ANY BOOK

Remembering the chapter headings and subchapter titles of an entire book is really easy with the memory system. If you know the chapter headings and the subchapter titles and you read the book, you can generally articulate the entire book.

1. Highlight or write the name of each chapter.

2. Convert the name of each chapter to an audionym(s).

3. Using the Cube, in location 1, see the audionym for chapter 1. In location 2, see the audionym for chapter 2. Do this for all the chapter headings before starting the subchapter headings.

4. Highlight or write the name of each subchapter heading for chapter 1.

5. Convert the name of each subchapter to an audionym(s).

6. Link the audionym for the first subchapter heading to the audionym in location 1 (chapter 1). Link the audionym for the second subchapter heading to the audionym for the first subchapter heading.

7. Repeat items 4, 5, and 6 for chapters 2, 3, 4, and so on.

This is an excellent memory exercise, and it is a very practical application of the memory system. There are numerous valuable uses of this application in the classroom and in business.

I can remember using this application many years ago in a corporate setting. At an executive staff meeting several months earlier, there had been a heated discussion (and disagreement) on a certain point. That evening I did some extensive research on the subject. I used the memory system to mentally lock in enough information to easily win any future debate on the subject if the opportunity were ever to arise again. Sure enough, the opportunity arose again several months later.

The individual who earlier had convinced everyone (but me) that he was correct didn't have a chance. He was about to argue the point again when I politely interrupted him. In a very calm, deliberate, and confident manner, I was able to provide research-based information that proved him wrong. Although I used less than 10 percent of the information I had stored in my mind, I was able to refer to multiple publications, books, and manuals by chapter, subchapters, and even page numbers and verbatim quotes—all without any notes. Needless to say, he was dumbfounded! More important, I think that, after that, the entire staff would have believed almost anything I said. They talked about it for a long time.

To gain a competitive edge in the classroom or on the job, use a combination of the memory tools you have learned in this book. Although the subjects will vary greatly, the system will remain relatively the same. And remember that no matter how complex the information may be, you will never work with more than two objects at a time.

HOW TO GET HIGHER GRADES
WITH LESS STUDY TIME

If you are a student, you now have a way to achieve higher grades in less study time. By using various combinations of the techniques you have learned in this book, you now have the tools you need to make learning a lot faster and a lot easier. Best of all, you will remember what you learn.

Simply select the appropriate tools for each memory task. I will share with you numerous actual applications to show you how to effectively apply these exciting new mental tools.

No matter what subject you are studying, it is almost a certainty that some combination of the tools you have learned in this book can easily be applied to it. Most information you mentally process falls into only three categories: words, numbers, and things that are already visual.

Please keep in mind that you must change information you want to remember into something you can see. If the information is words, use audionyms. If it is numbers, use the Number Code. If it is already visual, it is already easy to mentally process.

Converting words and numbers to visual images is only part of the process. After you can see the information in pictures, you must have a place to store it in your mind. This is why you must always have a known to work with. The known must also be something you can see. With this system, you never need to work with more than two pictures at a time: the known and the information you want to remember. The known can be a Cube or Grid location, an audionym, a face, a painting, or anything you are certain you will remember at the time you need to recall the information you are learning.

Even information as seemingly complex as the periodic table of the elements in chemistry can easily be broken down so that you work with only two objects at a time: one object represents what you know already—the known—and the other represents the information you want to learn.

TERMINOLOGY, NOMENCLATURE, TECHNICAL TERMS, AND VOCABULARY

For each of these categories, use the audionym technique and association. Change the word you are learning to an audionym. Then change the meaning to an audionym or audionyms. Associate the audionym(s) of the meaning with the audionym of the word you are learning. Later, when you see or hear the word, just change it to its audionym. Recall the audionym that was associated with it and you will recall the meaning of the word.

Biology: chromatid
Change chromatid to an audionym. For example, visualize a
  chrome mat.
Definition: A chromatid is one-half of a replicated chromosome.
Change the definition to audionyms. For example, replicated
  becomes *replica* and chromosome changes to a *chrome stone.*

Association: On the *chrome mat* see one-half of a replica (replicated) of a chrome stone (chromosome).

A chromatid is one-half of a replicated chromosome.

If you are studying biology, you will already be familiar with many of the terms. This will make it even easier to create audionyms for terms and definitions.

Simply by reviewing the new word, its audionym, its association, and its meaning several times, you won't need the memory techniques anymore. You'll just know the meaning of the word. Think of the memory techniques as a means to an end. Through use of the techniques and through use of the word, the need for the techniques disappears. What remains is knowledge.

HISTORY

For the history of any nation, there are, essentially, only three things you need to know:

1. Who was the leader?
2. When was the person the leader?
3. What happened when the person was the leader?

Use the following steps, in sequence, to learn the chronological history of any nation:

1. Change the name of the leader to an audionym.

2. Associate the audionym of the leader's name with location 1 in your first room.

3. Change the year the leader entered office to a Code Word, using the Number Code.

4. Associate the Code Word of the year with the audionym of the leader's name.

5. Change the first event of the leader's term to an audionym(s).

6. Associate the audionym for the first event of the leader's term with the Code Word for the year the leader entered office.

7. Repeat steps 5 and 6, associating (linking) the audionym for each event with the audionym for the previous event. You can link as many events as are needed for each leader.

If there is an extensive number of events for a leader, then each numbered room location can be used for a different event. Or each numbered room location can be used for a decade with links representing the major events of that decade.

This system is quite flexible and can be easily adjusted to your particular needs or to any application. Using a combination of only the techniques you learned in this book, you can remember virtually anything.

HOW TO MENTALLY CONVERT
KILOMETERS TO MILES

*Here is an amazingly simple method to convert kilometers to miles. I de-*veloped it during a trip to Europe in 1984. Select a "kilometers room." Mentally face the front wall. Follow these simple steps:

At location 1 (back left corner) see a gigantic **shoe**!

At location 2 (left wall) see a **tuna** leaping through the wall!

At location 3 (front left corner) see a gigantic child's **top** spinning!

At location 4 (front wall) see a huge **nail** stuck in the wall!

At location 5 (front right corner) see a huge **mat** (doormat) hanging in the corner!

At location 6 (right wall) see a gigantic **mike** (microphone) stuck in the wall!

At location 7 (back right corner) see a **ram** leaping out of the corner!

At location 8 (back wall) see a **lasso** flying out of the wall!

At location 9 (floor) see a gigantic **lily** bursting and growing out of the floor!

Imagine that each numbered room location has a zero to the right of it. The room, therefore, is numbered 10, 20, 30, 40, and so forth. The numbered room locations represent kilometers. The objects we placed in the numbered locations represent miles.

Location	Kilometers	Association	Miles (Approx.)
10 (back left corner)	10	shoe	6
20 (left wall)	20	tuna	12
30 (front left corner)	30	top	19
40 (front wall)	40	nail	25
50 (front right corner)	50	mat	31
60 (right wall)	60	mike	37
70 (back right corner)	70	ram	43
80 (back wall)	80	lasso	50
90 (floor)	90	lily	55

To mentally convert single-digit kilometers to miles, just slide the decimal point one position to the left.

Location	Kilometers	Association	Miles (Approx.)
1 (back left corner)	1.0	shoe	.6
2 (left wall)	2.0	tuna	1.2
3 (front left corner)	3.0	top	1.9
4 (front wall)	4.0	nail	2.5
5 (front right corner)	5.0	mat	3.1
6 (right wall)	6.0	mike	3.7
7 (back right corner)	7.0	ram	4.3

Location	Kilometers	Association	Miles (Approx.)
8 (back wall)	8.0	lasso	5.0
9 (floor)	9.0	lily	5.5

To convert three-digit kilometers to miles, just slide the decimal point one position to the right:

Location	Kilometers	Association	Miles (Approx.)
100 (back left corner)	100	shoe	60
200 (left wall)	200	tuna	120
300 (front left corner)	300	top	190
400 (front wall)	400	nail	250
500 (front right corner)	500	mat	310
600 (right wall)	600	mike	370
700 (back right corner)	700	ram	430
800 (back wall)	800	lasso	500
900 (floor)	900	lily	550

Notice that the pictures for units of kilometers and hundreds of kilometers remain the same. As long as you remember that the kilometer room is set up in tens or hundreds, rather than in units, it is easy to mentally slide the decimal point to accommodate units, hundreds, thousands, and so on.

To convert 444 kilometers to miles:
Convert the hundreds: 400 km = 250 miles
Convert the tens: 40 km = 25 miles
Convert the units: 4 km = 2.5 miles
Add the miles: 250 + 25 + 2.5 = 277.5 miles

Typically, however, you will not need to be so precise as to even use the units column. In the previous example, you would most likely convert 444 kilometers to "approximately 275 miles."

This is a very practical application. I suggest you use it every time you see or read distances in kilometers.

HOW TO LEARN
VERBATIM INFORMATION

I have worked with thousands of individuals who want and need to learn verbatim information. For most people, learning verbatim information is difficult, boring, and very time-consuming. With this system, however, it is fast and easy.

Verbatim information is required by actors, public speakers (especially when quoting others), and fraternal organizations requiring absolute accuracy in the conferral of ritualistic degrees.

In one application of my system, I applied the techniques to a presentation of more than 8,000 words of unusual and sometimes ancient grammar that required absolute accuracy. By absolute accuracy, I mean that every word had to be exactly right, including singular and plural words.

The more than 8,000-word presentation had been handed down through centuries and was not available in print. Yet, the accuracy required by the organization was so precise that a single word or a part of a word mispronounced or misplaced would be instantly detected by those in the organization who, themselves, had spent years learning the approximately one-hour presentation. What normally required many months or years to learn was accomplished by many members of the organization in only thirty-five to forty hours using a combination of the techniques you have learned in this book. It is unlikely that any verbatim application you will ever require will approach the difficulty of that presentation.

To show you how I apply the system to verbatim information, I'll use just part of the Gettysburg Address. The first step is to break the speech down to just a couple of words per line. It is very important to know that you would seldom need to break any text down as much as I have broken it down here. In fact, sometimes a single word will trigger a complete sentence in your mind without needing to break the sentence down at all.

Also, although you may need to break a text down into short lines initially, as you practice the presentation, you will need fewer audionyms and, in turn, fewer lines. You must always start with the known. In this case, the known is Lincoln's Gettysburg Address, so start by seeing Lincoln.

Always use your natural memory and common sense in learning anything with the memory system. There are many words such as *a, an, to, the, in, on,* and so on that just make sense in context and, therefore, you will not need an audionym to remember them.

Text	Audionyms
Fourscore	four scoreboards
and seven years ago	seven ears
our fathers	hourglass-fathers
brought forth	bratwurst-fort
upon this continent,	a pond-thistle-cotton-net
a new nation,	newt-nacho
conceived in Liberty,	cone-sieve-Liberty Bell
and dedicated	dead cat
to the proposition	two propellers

Text	Audionyms
that all men	almond
are created equal.	crate-a quail

Start with **Lincoln.**

See **Lincoln** holding **four scoreboards**! (fourscore)

The **scoreboards** have **seven ears** on them! (and seven years ago)

Each of the **seven ears** has an **hourglass** with **fathers** standing on it! (our fathers)

The **fathers** are holding a **bratwurst** with a **fort** on it! (brought forth)

The **fort** has **a pond** with a **thistle** sticking out of it! The **thistle** has **cotton** with a **net** on it! (upon this continent)

The **net** has a **newt** eating a **nacho** in it! (new nation)

See the **nacho** with a **cone** in it! The **cone** has a **sieve** in it! The **sieve** has the **Liberty Bell** in it! (conceived in Liberty)

On the **Liberty Bell** is a **cat** playing **dead**! (dedicated)

The **dead cat** stands up and holds **two propellers**! (to the proposition)

The **two propellers** have **almonds** all over them! (that all men)

The **almonds** have a **crate of quails** sitting on them! (are created equal)

Again, if you are learning this or any other presentation verbatim, you will find that, soon, you will not need many of the audionyms and that one or two audionyms will be enough to trigger one or more sentences. Try it! You'll be pleased with your results!

The above speech (as far as it is given) uses twenty audionyms. The same speech (as far as it is shown and as one becomes familiar with it) can be presented with only one audionym: **four scoreboards.** However, it is best to use more audionyms at first so you learn each sentence verbatim. Then, when you know the sentence, a single audionym will trigger the sentence or sentences.

Following is the Gettysburg Address highlighting the words and audionyms I ultimately used as memory aids to recall the entire speech.

Four scoreboards: *Four score and seven years ago our fathers brought forth on this continent, a new nation, conceived in Liberty, and dedicated to the proposition that all men are created equal.*

Engagement ring: *Now we are **engaged** in a great civil war, testing whether that nation, or any nation so conceived, and so dedicated, can long endure.*

Metal: *We are **met** on a great battlefield of that war. We have come to dedicate a portion of it as a final resting place for those who here gave their lives that that nation might live.*

Feet: *It is altogether **fitting** and proper that we should do this. But, in a larger sense, we can not dedicate—we can not consecrate—we can not hallow—this ground.*

Brave men (soldiers): *The **brave men**, living and dead, who struggled here, have consecrated it far above our poor power to add or detract.*

World (Globe): *The **world** will little note nor long remember what we say here, but it can never forget what they did here.*

Forest, tea leaf: *It is **for us the living**, rather, to be dedicated here to the unfinished work which they have, thus far, so nobly carried on.*

Rat: *It is **rather** for us to be here dedicated to the great task remaining before us—that from these honored dead we take increased devotion to that cause for which they gave the last full measure of devotion . . .*

Thatch roof, weed, hearing and: *. . . **that we here** highly resolve that these dead shall not have died in vain . . .*

Thistle, gnat: *. . . that **this nation,** under God, shall have a new birth of freedom—and that this government of the people, by the people, for the people, shall not perish from the earth.*

MENTAL EXERCISES
FOR MENTAL ALERTNESS

*Psychologists recommend that to stay mentally alert, we should do cross-*word puzzles, read, play cards, and engage in other challenging games. While these may be helpful mental activities, they pale in comparison to the advantages of using the organized techniques you have learned in this book. Here are a few things that, with just a little practice, will enable you to astound yourself, your family, your friends, and anyone you meet. Best of all, it will continually sharpen your mind.

1. Have someone give you a list of twenty, forty, or sixty numbers two digits at a time. Use the Number Code, the Cube, and association to recall them forward, in reverse order, and randomly.

2. Make a set of one hundred flash cards numbered zero zero through ninety-nine and practice recalling the numbers yourself

3. Have someone give you a list of ten, twenty, or thirty randomly numbered items.

4. Make a set of flash cards with random words and practice recalling the words.

5. Learn and practice the Tour of the Knight.

6. Practice recalling ten, twenty, thirty, or an entire deck of
   playing cards.

If you have carefully followed all of the steps in this learning
system, you should feel justifiably proud of your accomplishment.
It is always difficult to dramatically change the way we do anything—
including remembering. I congratulate you on your willingness to
explore the untapped natural resources of your mind. I guarantee
you that if you continue this memory exploration you will reap
countless rewards for the rest of your life!

TEACH YOUR CHILD HOW TO REMEMBER

Next to love and respect, what finer gift could you give your
child than the gift of learning how to remember? Many parents are
now using this system to teach their children the presidents and
their terms of office, the states and the dates they entered the
Union, U.S. geography, world geography, music theory, the multiplication facts, and so much more.

Every time your child uses this system to learn anything, they
strengthen their ability to remember. It also makes them realize
that it is much easier to use an organized system to learn things
than it is to use the antiquated and inefficient method of repetition.

Start by having your child use the numbered Cube to learn just
five or ten items. Build from there and you will be amazed at how
quickly and easily your child will learn with this organized system.
Let us hear about your successes!

TEN MORE EVERYDAY
APPLICATIONS AND EXERCISES

There are many everyday applications that are short, fast, and very practical. Following are ten examples of applications of the system that you may find most useful.

1. Your son and/or daughter plays soccer. You would like to know the name of each of his/her teammates and the names of their parent(s).

   a. Get a list of all the team members and the names of their parents.
   b. Change the name of each player to an audionym. For example, Madaline to *mandolin.*
   c. Select a familiar room for the names of the first nine teammates.
   d. At location 1 (the back left corner), see the mandolin, at location 2 (the left wall), see the audionym for the next teammate, and so on.
   e. Change the name of each parent to an audionym. For example, Madaline's mother's name is Teresa; imagine *trees.* Just see the mandolin with trees growing out of it!

Later when you think of location 1, you'll see the mandolin with the trees. That will remind you that the player's name is Madaline and her mother's name is Teresa.

f. If the father's name is Larry, picture a *lariat*. See the mandolin with the trees, then see the trees with a gigantic lariat around them! Mandolin, trees, lariat: Madaline, Teresa, Larry. Repeat the process at each numbered location. When you get to location 9, select a 10s room and start at the ceiling with location 10, then the back left corner with location 11, and so on.

As a mental exercise, practice recalling the names of all the teammates and their parents. Use the system for remembering names and visualize the teammates and their parents as you practice reviewing their names.

2. Prepare a list of things to purchase at a grocery store or at a drugstore. Use the Cube method to learn the list. Take the list with you as a backup, but don't use it unless you need to. After you finish shopping, you may wish to check the list to confirm that you purchased everything on the list. Soon, however, you won't need to take a list with you. This is an excellent mental exercise and one that will help keep you mentally alert for a lifetime.

3. Here is an application I used to do during my presentations to large groups. I would memorize the contents of a current issue of a popular magazine. Then during my presentation I would have the audience pass the magazine around. Someone would give me a page number and I would tell them what was on that page. Sometimes someone would tell me

what was on the page and I would give them the page number. This is another great memory exercise—just for fun.

Using any magazine, look at the contents of page 1 and associate the contents with location 1 in your Units room (zero to nine room). Next, look at page 2 and associate the contents with location 2 in your Units room. Continue to page 9. Then associate the contents of page 10 with location 10 (the ceiling) of your 10s room.

To further impress your family and friends, you can pay attention to the finer details of what is located on a page of a magazine. I remember a page of a magazine that had a dollar bill with the serial number very visible. It was most impressive to recall the serial number of the dollar bill.

4. Once, while sitting in the lobby of a corporate office waiting for my scheduled appointment, I noticed the mission statement and corporate objectives of the organization on a framed poster on the wall. Naturally, I incorporated that into my presentation to the vice-president with whom I met. She seemed more impressed with that than she was with the rest of my presentation. She even had me demonstrate it to several other officers before I left the building. Oh, yes, and she scheduled my memory training for her entire executive staff. Every opportunity to exercise your mind is worthwhile. Some of those opportunities can turn into great rewards.

5. When traveling, especially on interstate highways, a good mental exercise is to memorize the names (towns) of the exits and their mileage markers. It is fun, easy, and practical. It is also a great mental exercise. Start with room location 1 and place the audionym for the town in that location. Then

convert the mile marker to a Code Word and link it to the audionym for the town.

If the exits are numbered sequentially, 1, 2, 3, and so on, use the numbered room system for the exit numbers. Link the audionym for each town to the room location for the exit number. Then convert the mile marker to a Code Word and link it to the audionym for the town.

6. Learn your credit card numbers, expiration dates, and any related codes. Create a visual image for each credit card as the known (a place to start). Then change the numbers to Code Words and link them together. Review the numbers immediately, then the next day, then the next week, and so on. When asked for your credit card number, develop the habit of giving it from memory.

7. It is not practical to mentally store hundreds of recipes. It is practical, however, to mentally store a few food or drink recipes that you may make frequently. For a food or drink recipe, change the name of the food or drink into an audionym. If the food or drink is already something you can visualize, just use that visual image. Then, if the ingredients are not already things you can easily see or imagine, change them to audionyms and link them together in sequence. Use *tea* for teaspoon, *table* for tablespoon, and so on. For quantities, use *one fork* for ¼, *one tree* for ⅓, *one half-dollar* for ½, and *three forks* for ¾.

Buttermilk Cornbread

1 cup all-purpose flour
1 cup yellow cornmeal

¼ cup granulated sugar
1 tablespoon baking powder
1 teaspoon baking soda
3 tablespoons butter, melted
1⅓ cups buttermilk
1 large egg

Select a room for the ingredients and see buttermilk cornbread covering the ceiling.

In location 1, see one cup of all-purpose flour (1 cup all-purpose flour).

In location 2, see one cup of yellow cornmeal (1 cup yellow cornmeal).

In location 3, see one fork with a cup of granulated sugar on it (¼ cup granulated sugar).

In location 4, see a table with baking powder all over it (1 tablespoon baking powder).

In location 5, see one cup of tea with baking soda floating in it (1 teaspoon baking soda).

In location 6, see three tables with melted butter all over them (three tablespoons of melted butter)

In location 7, see one cup of buttermilk, and beside it one tree with a cup of buttermilk in it (1⅓ cups buttermilk).

In location 8 see a large egg.

1. Preheat the oven to 425°F.

Memory technique: in the next room, at location 1, see an *oven* with *rooms* in it! (Oven set at 430°.)

2. Butter an 8-inch square *baking pan*; set it aside.

Memory technique: in location 2, see an 8-inch square baking pan with butter in it standing on its side. (Butter an 8-inch square *baking pan*; set it aside.)

3. In a bowl, stir together the flour, cornmeal, sugar, *baking* powder, and baking soda.

Memory technique: in location 3, see a bowl with an electric mixer in it. It is stirring the contents of locations 1 through 5 from the previous room in it. (In a bowl, stir together flour, cornmeal, sugar, *baking* powder, and baking soda.)

4. In a *small bowl*, stir together butter and buttermilk with an electric mixer at low speed. Beat in egg.

Memory technique: in location 4, see a *small bowl* with an electric mixer in it. It is stirring the butter and buttermilk, then the egg (the contents of locations 6,7, and 8 in the previous room). (In a *small bowl*, stir together butter and buttermilk with an electric mixer at low speed. Beat in egg.)

5. Mix all ingredients and stir only until combined.

Memory technique: in location 5, see a huge bowl with all the ingredients mixed together.

6. Pour batter into prepared *pan* and bake for 30 minutes or until golden-brown.

Memory technique: at location 6, see the batter in the prepared *pan* in the oven with a *moose* standing guard outside until it turns golden brown. (Pour batter into prepared *pan* and bake for 30 minutes or until golden-brown.)

8. Let's suggest that you eat out often. You may have visited the same restaurants for several years and have been served by the same servers, but you don't know their names. That may be because, until now, you did not realize that you could. Start today to make a point of remembering the names of

your waiters. You will be amazed with your success and even more amazed with the remarkably better service you receive. As an added memory exercise, you may wish to start a mental link of the names of the waiters whose names you learn at each restaurant.

9. To remember the names and times of TV shows, first make a list of the programs of interest to you for the seven days of the week. Change the name of each day of the week to an audionym.

Monday becomes *moon*
Tuesday becomes *tooth*
Wednesday becomes *wedding*
Thursday becomes *thirsty* (glass of water)
Friday becomes *fried egg*
Saturday becomes *Saturn* (the planet)
Sunday becomes *sun*

Use seven rooms—one for each day of the week—and see each of the seven audionyms at the ceiling of each of the seven rooms.

You can then mentally store nine programs for each of the seven days of the week:

a. Change the name of the first program to an audionym and see it in location in the appropriate room.
b. Convert the number of the channel to a Code Word and link it to the audionym for the name of the program.
c. Convert the time of the program to a Code Word and link it to the Code Word for the channel.

Repeat a, b, and c, for the time and channel of any program on any day of the week.

10. To know the number of calories in food items, make a list of ten foods. Visualize each food item. There is no need to create an audionym for the food items because they are objects you can see.

Look up the caloric content of each item. Change the number of calories in each food item to a Code Word using the Number Code. Associate the Code Word (illogically) with the food item.

After you learn the number of calories in the ten food items, repeat the process with ten more foods at a time. It is quite easy to learn the number of calories in any number of foods.

On the following pages are 1,000 Key Words. The Key Words are used to remember the numbers 0 through 999. There is no need to memorize the Code Words. Just use this dictionary when you need to remember any number between 0 and 999.

0	ice, hose, sea
1	tie, toe, tea, hat
2	Noah, knee, hen
3	Ma, mow, ham
4	row, rye, oar, hair
5	oil, whale, heel
6	shoe, show, hash
7	key, cow, hook
8	tee, toe, hoof
9	pie, pea, hoop
10	toes, ties, hats
11	tote (bag), tot, toad
12	tuna, tin, teen
13	team, tam, tomb

14   tire, tear, tour, water
15   tail, tool, towel
16   dish, dash, ditch
17   tack, teak, duck
18   TV, taffy, dove
19   top, tip, teepee, tub

20   nose, niece, anis
21   net, knit, knot
22   nanny, nun, noon
23   name (plate)
24   new oar, Nero
25   nail, knoll, Nile
26   notch, new shoe, wench
27   new key, neck
28   knife, Navy
29   knob, nap (a bed)

30   moose, mice, maze
31   meat, mat, mud
32   moon, man, money
33   Mom, mummy
34   mower, mare
35   mail, mule, meal
36   match, mush
37   mike, mug
38   muff, movie
39   map, mop

40   rose, rice, race
41   rat, root, wreath
42   rain, run, wren

43 ram, room, ream
44 rower, rear
45 rail, reel, roll, rule
46 roach, rash
47 rock, rug, rag
48 roof, reef
49 rope, robe

50 lasso, lace
51 light, lot, loot, lead
52 lion, line
53 lime, loom
54 lure, lair
55 lily, lolli(pop)
56 leash, latch
57 lake, leek, lock
58 leaf, loaf
59 lip, loop, lab

60 cheese, chess, juice
61 chute, sheet, shot
62 chain, chin
63 chime, jam, gem
64 chair, cherry, jar
65 shell, chili, jelly
66 choo-choo, judge
67 chalk, cheek, jack, check
68 chef, chief, chive
69 chip, ship, sheep

70 case, keys, gas
71 coat, kit, cot, cat

72   cone, can, cane
73   comb, game, cam
74   car, core, gear
75   coal, claw, gill
76   cash, quiche
77   cake, Coke
78   cuff, cave, cove
79   cap, cup, cape

80   face, fuse, fez
81   foot, food, vat
82   phone, fan, fin
83   foam, fume
84   fur, fire, fair
85   file, foil, fly
86   fish, fudge
87   fog, fig, vac
88   fife
89   fob

90   pies, peas, bus
91   bait, beet, boat, bat
92   pane, pine, pin
93   pom-(pom), beam
94   pear, pier, bear
95   pale, pill, poll, pool
96   peach, bush
97   peak, book, bike
98   puff, beef
99   pipe, peep, pop, bib

KEY WORDS 000 THROUGH 049

000	ice houses	025	snail
001	icy sod	026	snatch
002	season	027	snake
003	sesame	028	sniff
004	scissor	029	snap
005	sizzle (steak)	030	seams
006	sausage	031	summit
007	icy sock	032	salmon
008	ice safe	033	seam hem
009	ice sub	034	swimmer
010	seeds	035	sawmill
011	studio	036	smash
012	stein	037	smoke
013	steam	038	sew muff
014	star	039	swamp
015	stool	040	seahorse
016	stage	041	sword
017	steak	042	siren
018	stove	043	serum
019	step	044	zero hour
020	signs	045	cereal
021	sand	046	search
022	sign-in	047	ice rack
023	cinema	048	surf
024	snare	049	syrup

KEY WORDS 050 THROUGH 099

050	seals	075	school
051	salt	076	sketch
052	saloon	077	ice cake
053	slum	078	scuff
054	sailor	079	scuba
055	seal oil	080	sieves
056	sledge	081	soffit
057	silk	082	siphon
058	slave	083	sea foam
059	slip	084	savior
060	switches	085	swivel
061	associate	086	savage
062	session	087	civic
063	ice jam	088	safe-ivy
064	seashore	089	safe-pie
065	seashell	090	space
066	wise judge	091	spade
067	ice check	092	spoon
068	switch off	093	spam
069	ice ship	094	spur
070	skis	095	spool
071	skate	096	speech
072	skin	097	spoke
073	Eskimo	098	soup-ivy
074	cigar	099	soup-pea

KEY WORDS 100 THROUGH 149

100	thesis	125	tunnel
101	toast	126	tonnage
102	dozen	127	tonic
103	toss 'em	128	the Navy
104	dozer	129	tune-up
105	tassel	130	teams
106	dosage	131	tomato
107	tusk	132	domino
108	toes–ivy	133	time me
109	toss–up	134	timer
110	tights	135	tamale
111	tote-tie	136	tie-match
112	titan	137	tomahawk
113	totem	138	tie-movie
114	tutor	139	dump
115	title	140	dress
116	toe touch	141	treat
117	tie tack	142	train
118	taffy	143	drum
119	hot tub	144	drawer
120	tennis	145	drill
121	tent	146	trash
122	tune in	147	truck
123	the name	148	drive
124	tanner	149	trap

KEY WORDS 150 THROUGH 199

150	tools	175	tackle
151	toilet	176	hat–cash
152	tall hen	177	hat–cake
153	tall home	178	hat–cuff
154	tailor	179	teacup
155	tall whale	180	hat–fez
156	tall shoe	181	divot
157	tail–key	182	Tiffany
158	tail–hoof	183	hat–foam
159	tulip	184	diver
160	duchess	185	hat–file
161	tee shot	186	hat–fish
162	hat–chain	187	hat–fig
163	hat–chime	188	hat–fife
164	teacher	189	hat–fob
165	hat–shell	190	tepees
166	hat–judge	191	hat–bat
167	hat–chalk	192	hat pin
168	hat–chef	193	hat–pom (pom)
169	hat–ship	194	hat–pear
170	tacks	195	table
171	ticket	196	hat–peach
172	token	197	hat–book
173	hat–comb	198	hat–beef
174	dagger	199	hat–pipe

KEY WORDS 200 THROUGH 249

200	nieces	225	Union Hall
201	nest	226	new notch
202	ensign	227	hen-neck
203	new seam	228	new knife
204	answer	229	new knob
205	nozzle	230	names
206	new sash	231	inmate
207	new sock	232	honeymoon
208	new safe	233	new mama
209	newsboy	234	new hammer
210	nuts	235	enamel
211	knitted	236	new match
212	Indian	237	new hammock
213	anatomy	238	nymph
214	notary	239	new map
215	needle	240	nurse
216	new dish	241	north
217	antique	242	new horn
218	native	243	new room
219	windup	244	honorary
220	onions	245	new reel
221	noon tea	246	new arch
222	nun-hen	247	wine rack
223	new name	248	nerve
224	nunnery	249	new rope

KEY WORDS 250 THROUGH 299

250	nails	275	nickel
251	inlet	276	new cash
252	nylon	277	new cake
253	new lamb	278	new calf
254	inhaler	279	hen coop
255	Honolulu	280	invoice
256	new leash	281	no fat (milk)
257	new lock	282	new phone
258	new leaf	283	new foam
259	new lab	284	new fur
260	inches	285	navel
261	new sheet	286	new fish
262	engine	287	new vac(uum)
263	new chime	288	new fife
264	new chair	289	new fob
265	new shell	290	new bus
266	new judge	291	new pet
267	new jug	292	new pan
268	anchovy	293	new bomb
269	new ship	294	neighbor
270	new keys	295	nipple
271	nugget	296	new beach
272	new cane	297	new book
273	honeycomb	298	new beef
274	anchor	299	new pipe

KEY WORDS 300 THROUGH 349

300	Moses	325	manual
301	mist	326	moon-shoe
302	mason	327	maniac
303	museum	328	my knife
304	miser	329	my knob
305	missile	330	memos
306	massage	331	my mat
307	mask	332	my money
308	my safe	333	my mummy
309	my soap	334	mummer
310	maids	335	mammal
311	my tote	336	my match
312	mitten	337	my mug
313	madam	338	my muff
314	motor	339	my mop
315	motel	340	Morse (code)
316	my dish	341	mart
317	medic	342	Marine
318	my TV	343	my room
319	my tape	344	mirror
320	mayonnaise	345	mural
321	mint	346	march
322	moon-hen	347	mark
323	my name	348	my roof
324	miner	349	my robe

KEY WORDS 350 THROUGH 399

350	miles		375	my goal
351	mallet		376	my cash
352	melon		377	my cake
353	my lamb		378	my coffee
354	mailer		379	makeup
355	mole hill		380	movies
356	mileage		381	my foot
357	milk		382	muffin
358	ham loaf		383	my foam
359	mail boy		384	mover
360	matches		385	muffle
361	machete		386	my fish
362	machine		387	moving (van)
363	my jam		388	muff-ivy
364	major		389	my fob
365	my shell		390	embassy
366	mesh shoe		391	my pet
367	magic		392	ham bone
368	my chef		393	my poem
369	my ship		394	umpire
370	mugs		395	maple
371	my coat		396	my beach
372	my gun		397	hymnbook
373	my gum		398	my puff
374	my car		399	my baby

KEY WORDS 400 THROUGH 449

400	roses	425	renewal
401	roast	426	ranch
402	raisin	427	hairy neck
403	resume	428	runoff
404	razor	429	rainbow
405	wrestle	430	rooms
406	horseshoe	431	remote
407	rescue	432	Roman
408	rice-hoof	433	our Mom
409	recipe	434	roamer
410	rats	435	airmail
411	rotate	436	rummage
412	red hen	437	ram-key
413	red ham	438	ram-hoof
414	radar	439	ramp
415	rattle	440	rowers
416	radish	441	reward
417	riding	442	rerun
418	red ivy	443	hairy arm
419	write-up	444	rare oar
420	ruins	445	rural
421	rent	446	rare show
422	reunion	447	rare key
423	uranium	448	wire roof
424	runner	449	wire rope

KEY WORDS 450 THROUGH 499

450	rolls	475	oracle
451	roulette	476	wreckage
452	airline	477	rocking (chair)
453	heirloom	478	rake off
454	ruler	479	rack up
455	reel-whale	480	roofs
456	relish	481	raft
457	relic	482	earphone
458	wire leaf	483	roof-ham
459	roll up (pant)	484	river
460	riches	485	rifle
461	rigid	486	refugee
462	Russian	487	roof-key
463	Hiroshima	488	roof-fife
464	archer	489	roof-pie
465	rich oil	490	robes
466	hairy judge	491	rabbit
467	rich guy	492	robin
468	air chief	493	air bomb
469	airship	494	arbor
470	rugs	495	ripple
471	rocket	496	rubbish
472	organ	497	wire-book
473	war game	498	wire-puff
474	rocker	499	wire-pipe

KEY WORDS 500 THROUGH 549

500	lassos	525	Lionel
501	list	526	lounge
502	lesson	527	link
503	wholesome	528	yellow knife
504	laser	529	lineup
505	wholesale	530	limes
506	yellow sash	531	limit (speed)
507	Alaska	532	lemon
508	yellow sofa	533	yellow mummy
509	oily soap	534	yellow mower
510	lighthouse	535	yellow mule
511	Yuletide	536	yellow match
512	Latin	537	yellow mug
513	yellow team	538	yellow muff
514	ladder	539	lamp
515	ladle	540	walrus
516	old shoe	541	yellow rod
517	yellow dog	542	yellow rain
518	yellow TV	543	alarm
519	yellow top	544	yellow rower
520	lens	545	laurel
521	land	546	yellow roach
522	linen	547	lark
523	holy name	548	yellow roof
524	lunar	549	yellow rope

KEY WORDS 550 THROUGH 599

550	lilies	575	legal (paper)
551	lily-tea	576	luggage
552	lily-hen	577	lock-key
553	lily-ham	578	lock-ivy
554	lily-lure	579	lock-pie
555	lily-whale	580	leaves
556	yellow leash	581	loft
557	lilac	582	loaf-wine
558	lily-ivy	583	loaf-ham
559	lullaby	584	lever
560	eyelashes	585	level
561	leash-tie	586	loaf-shoe
562	lotion	587	loaf-key
563	leash-ham	588	loaf-ivy
564	wheelchair	589	loaf-pie
565	yellow shell	590	lips
566	leash-shoe	591	low bed
567	leash-key	592	Alpine
568	leash-ivy	593	album
569	leash-pie	594	labor
570	locks	595	lapel
571	locket	596	whale-beach
572	log-hen	597	law book
573	welcome (mat)	598	whale-puff
574	locker	599	whale-pipe

KEY WORDS 600 THROUGH 649

600	cheeses	625	channel
601	chest	626	change
602	shoes-hen	627	shiny key
603	shoes-ham	628	chain-ivy
604	juicer	629	chain-pie
605	chisel	630	chimes
606	shoe-sash	631	chime-tie
607	shoe-sock	632	watchman
608	shoe-safe	633	chime-ham
609	shoe-soap	634	chime-hair
610	shades	635	chime-whale
611	shoe-toad	636	chime-shoe
612	jitney	637	Jamaica
613	shoe-team	638	chime-ivy
614	shutter	639	jump
615	shuttle	640	shears
616	shoe-tissue	641	shirt
617	show dog	642	shrine
618	shoe-TV	643	charm
619	shoe-top	644	juror
620	chains	645	chair-whale
621	giant	646	church
622	shoe-nun	647	shark
623	chain-ham	648	sheriff
624	chain-hair	649	shrub

KEY WORDS 650 THROUGH 699

650	shells	675	shackle
651	jolt	676	check-shoe
652	shell-hen	677	check-key
653	shell-ham	678	check-ivy
654	jeweler	679	check-pie
655	shell-whale	680	chiefs
656	shell-shoe	681	chef-tie
657	shellac	682	chiffon
658	shelf	683	chef-ham
659	jalopy	684	chauffeur
660	judges	685	shovel
661	judge-tie	686	shoe-fish
662	shoeshine	687	chef-key
663	judge-ham	688	chef-ivy
664	judge-hair	689	watch fob
665	judge-whale	690	chips
666	judge-shoe	691	Egypt
667	judge-key	692	Japan
668	judge-ivy	693	ship-ham
669	judge-pie	694	chopper
670	checks	695	chapel
671	jacket	696	ship-shoe
672	chicken	697	ship-key
673	check-ham	698	ship-ivy
674	checker	699	ship-pie

KEY WORDS 700 THROUGH 749

700	cases	725	canal
701	cast	726	cone-shoe
702	cousin	727	cone-key
703	kiss-ham	728	convoy
704	geyser	729	canopy
705	castle	730	combs
706	case-shoe	731	comet
707	case-cow	732	comb-hen
708	case-ivy	733	comb-ham
709	case-pie	734	camera
710	kites	735	camel
711	cadet	736	comb-shoe
712	cotton	737	comb-key
713	academy	738	comb-ivy
714	guitar	739	camp
715	cattle	740	grass
716	cottage	741	crate
717	coat-cow	742	crayon
718	coat-ivy	743	cream
719	coat-pie	744	carrier
720	canes	745	grill
721	candy	746	crutch
722	cannon	747	creek
723	cone-ham	748	gravy
724	canary	749	grape

KEY WORDS 750 THROUGH 799

750	glass	775	goggle
751	cleat	776	cake-shoe
752	gallon	777	cake-key
753	clam	778	cake-ivy
754	collar	779	cake-cap
755	ukelele	780	caves
756	college	781	gift
757	clock	782	coffin
758	glove	783	cuff-ham
759	club	784	cover
760	coaches	785	gavel
761	gadget	786	hook-fish
762	caution (light)	787	cuff-key
763	coach 'em	788	cave-ivy
764	cashier	789	cuff-pie
765	eggshell	790	caboose
766	key-judge	791	keypad
767	cage-key	792	cabin
768	cage-hoof	793	cap-ham
769	ketchup	794	copper
770	cakes	795	cable
771	cooked	796	cabbage
772	cocoon	797	cap-key
773	gingham	798	cap-ivy
774	Quaker	799	cobweb

KEY WORDS 800 THROUGH 849

800	offices	825	funnel
801	fist	826	phone-shoe
802	fez-hen	827	phone-key
803	fez-ham	828	phone-ivy
804	visor	829	phone-pie
805	vessel	830	fumes
806	fez-shoe	831	foam-tie
807	fez-key	832	foam-hen
808	fez-ivy	833	foam-ham
809	fez-pie	834	femur
810	foot-ice	835	foam-whale
811	foot-tie	836	foam-shoe
812	foot-hen	837	foam-key
813	foot-ham	838	foam-ivy
814	fighter	839	foam-pie
815	fiddle	840	fries
816	footage	841	freight
817	foot-key	842	fern
818	foot-ivy	843	farm
819	foot-pie	844	fryer
820	fence	845	frill
821	vent	846	fur-shoe
822	phone-hen	847	frog
823	venom	848	fur-ivy
824	phone-hair	849	frappé

KEY WORDS 850 THROUGH 899

850	flies	875	vocal
851	fleet	876	fig-shoe
852	violin	877	fig-key
853	film	878	fig-ivy
854	flier	879	fig-cap
855	foil-whale	880	fife-ice
856	flash	881	fife-tie
857	flag	882	fife-hen
858	valve	883	fife-ham
859	flap (mud)	884	fife-hair
860	fishes	885	fife-whale
861	fish-tie	886	fife-shoe
862	fish-hen	887	fife-key
863	fish-ham	888	fife-ivy
864	fish-hair	889	fife-pie
865	fish-whale	890	fob-ice
866	fish-shoe	891	fob-tie
867	fishhook	892	fob-hen
868	fish-ivy	893	fob-ham
869	fish-pie	894	fob-hair
870	fox	895	fob-whale
871	fig-tie	896	fob-shoe
872	afghan	897	fob-key
873	vacuum	898	fob-ivy
874	fig-hair	899	fob-pie

KEY WORDS 900 THROUGH 949

900	bases	925	panel
901	bust	926	banjo
902	basin	927	bone-key
903	bosom	928	bone-ivy
904	bazaar	929	bone-pie
905	puzzle	930	beams
906	passage	931	beam-tie
907	bazooka	932	beam-hen
908	bus-ivy	933	beam-mummy
909	pea soup	934	beam-hair
910	boots	935	beam-whale
911	potato	936	beam-shoe
912	baton	937	beam-key
913	podium	938	beam-ivy
914	butter	939	pump
915	poodle	940	pears
916	pitch	941	bride
917	pudding	942	brain
918	bat-ivy	943	broom
919	potpie	944	prayer
920	bonus	945	Braille
921	bonnet	946	bridge
922	banana	947	brick
923	Panama	948	brave
924	banner	949	prop

KEY WORDS 950 THROUGH 999

950	bills	975	pickle
951	bolt	976	package
952	balloon	977	peacock
953	plum	978	book-ivy
954	blower	979	book-pie
955	bell-whale	980	beehives
956	bleach	981	puff-tie
957	block	982	puff-hen
958	bell-ivy	983	puff-ham
959	bulb	984	beaver
960	peaches	985	buffalo
961	budget	986	puff-shoe
962	pigeon	987	puff-key
963	pajama	988	puff-ivy
964	pitcher	989	puff-pie
965	bushel	990	pipes
966	peach-shoe	991	puppet
967	peach-key	992	baboon
968	peach-ivy	993	pipe-ham
969	peach pie	994	paper
970	bikes	995	Bible
971	pocket	996	pipe-shoe
972	bacon	997	pipe-key
973	pygmy	998	pipe-ivy
974	beggar	999	pipe-pie

Acknowledgments

*I would like to thank and congratulate the more than 2.5 million individu*als who have completed my applied learning systems with an overall average of above 95 percent retention. Because of them, the academic and business worlds are discovering the value and effectiveness of organized memory systems. Because of them, the learning revolution has begun!

I would also like to thank the many professional educators and administrators for their contributions in the development, piloting, and implementation of a number of my applied learning systems: Dr. Susan Collins; Dr. Marsha Zehner; Dr. Thomas Jenkins; Russel M. Sutton; Rosalie Virgo; and the thousands of teachers, professors, and corporate trainers who use my systems daily. Their progressive attitudes in seeking more effective methods of instruction and their commitment to raising the bar of academic excellence in America will help millions of students achieve unprecedented academic success with my learning systems.

I want to thank my friend and business associate, Robert Maddestra, President of DCM Instructional Systems, who has believed in and marketed my medical education series for more than twenty-five years. He helped lay the foundation to establish applied

ACKNOWLEDGMENTS

memory techniques both as a science and as a commercially successful enterprise. His integrity is beyond reproach. Best of all, I am most privileged that he is one of my very closest and trusted friends.

I would also like to thank Max Maxwell, my business associate, whose intellectual stimulation and vision of the future of education using my memory systems has been most inspiring.

About the Author

Dean Vaughn is a living testimony to the advantages of using his memory systems.

At an early age, he began work in an entry-level position at one of the largest health insurance companies in America. Within six and a half years, he had advanced through seven newly created positions to become the youngest vice president in the history of the company. With thirty-four years remaining until retirement, he gave up the security of his new position to begin to teach others the secrets of the Dean Vaughn Total Retention System. It is a decision for which more than two and a half million individuals are most appreciative.

Vaughn's interest in memory began near the North Pole while working as a civilian at the United States Ballistic Missile Early Warning System at Thule, Greenland. He had just completed two years of military service and had gone to Greenland as a civilian to earn enough money to pay for a college education. There he began the self-study of psychology that led him to an insatiable interest in memory. He traced memory systems and techniques to ancient times, and discovered that ancient scholars used organized memory systems with exceptional results.

Vaughn began to develop and test his own methods on his fellow workers. Soon he discovered that "the secret of the ages" could be applied even more effectively to the needs of modern society.

Today, Dean Vaughn is spearheading a learning revolution. He is the only author who has applied and validated memory techniques in practical academic and business applications. He has proven that his memory systems work—better than any known to exist.

The finest testimonial to the effectiveness of Dean Vaughn's methods is that he has revolutionized the teaching of every subject to which he has applied his learning system. Courses currently available include a wide range of subjects, such as the Vaughn Cube for Music Theory, the Vaughn Cube for Mathematics (addition, subtraction, multiplication, division), telling time, plane and solid geometry, U.S. and world geography, conversational Spanish, world language vocabulary, Latin and Greek for English vocabulary, the periodic table of chemical elements, the world's leading medical terminology course, basic human anatomy, dental terminology, anatomy, and physiology.

Remarkably, all of Dean Vaughn's applied learning systems are designed with an objective of 100 percent retention. His teaching aids are guaranteed to be the fastest, easiest, and most effective methods to teach the respective subject, or a full refund is offered. Even more remarkable, with more than twelve thousand schools, colleges, companies, hospitals, and government agencies having used these applied teaching aids, no refunds have ever been requested.

Dean Vaughn has been the keynote speaker for more than three hundred state, national, and international conventions of academic and business leaders, and he is consistently acclaimed as "the best we have ever had!"